THE WHEEL OF THINGS

The Wheel of Things

A biography of L.M. Montgomery
author of *Anne of Green Gables*

Mollie Gillen

Fitzhenry & Whiteside Limited

Where, then, is the River? My dream told
me to find it . . . . By it one attains freedom
from the Wheel of Things . . . .

—Rudyard Kipling
(*Kim*)

Contents

Preface and Acknowledgements

Maud Montgomery had many close friends, men and women both, but with two men she corresponded for forty-odd of her sixty-seven years. One of them, Ephraim Weber, a Canadian, she met briefly three times—in 1928, 1930 and 1935. The second, George Boyd MacMillan, a Scot, she met once only, when he and a friend accompanied her and her husband on a ten-day trip during her honeymoon visit to Scotland in 1911.

The letters she wrote to Weber were handed after his death to his former student and long-time friend Professor Wilfrid Eggleston and lodged in the Public Archives in Ottawa. When work on this book began, no one had tried to discover if her letters to George MacMillan had survived.

My attempt to locate them began with a letter to the Clackmannan County Librarian in Alloa, where I knew Mr MacMillan had lived. From there, through the kindness of many people, through a variety of searches—to find a will (and the name of a possible executor), to find a colleague (Mr. John Gardner, a fellow-reporter), and to find possible descendants or relatives—I was led to Mr George McMillan, son of George Boyd MacMillan's brother John, who lives with his sister Margaretha in Clackmannan.

And the miracle happened—the sort of miracle all biographers hope to experience. The letters had indeed survived, carefully fastened in folders in chronological order, and preserved in his uncle's trunk—the classic location for such undiscovered treasure—by Mr MacMillan's nephew (he has changed the spelling of his name, by local custom, to avoid confusion).

This collection (some eighty long letters, with postcards, clippings and briefer notes) will now find a home in Ottawa, available for future scholars who want to find out more about L. M. Montgomery. It has revealed much about her, although of course for this book much rich material has had to be reluctantly omitted. One fact of incidental but special interest emerges and is worth emphasizing: she wished to be known either as L. M. Montgomery or Maud Montgomery. "I was never in my life called 'Lucy Maud,' " she wrote. "My friends called me 'Maud' and nothing else." And she won her battle to have *Anne* published under the name L. M. Montgomery and not "Lucy Maud Montgomery which I loathe."

On her Island in summer, tourists drive the red roads through a landscape of field and sea and sky to visit Green Gables in its beautiful setting not far from where Maud Montgomery grew up "eleven miles from a railway and twenty-four miles from a town, but only half a mile from one of the finest sea-beaches in the world."

One of her monuments on Prince Edward Island is the National Park at Cavendish, its eighteen-hole golf course embracing the farms and fields, the lanes and woods she had loved so well. The other is the body of her work, especially *Anne of Green Gables,* still selling millions of copies in dozens of languages around the world. Mention Anne to any woman in English-speaking countries, and the reply, more often than not, will be, "I was brought up on her."

A plaque on the lawn of the Manse at Leaskdale erected by the Ontario Historic Sites Board in July 1965 commemorates Maud's residence there. In Charlottetown, Montgomery Hall was opened at Prince of Wales College in 1961 as a women's residence and student centre. In 1969 the Canadian National Railway renamed its 100-car ferry plying between New Brunswick and the Island the *Lucy Maud Montgomery.*

The old home of Maud's grandparents where she spent those magic years of growing up has been for a long time a heap of rubble, but the federal government has sponsored the restoration of a house of the period, opened in August 1973, "approximately 100 years old and an almost exact duplicate of the MacNeill home" to serve as the present Cavendish post office, with Mary Lowther, granddaughter of Maud's Uncle John as its first postmaster. It is unfortunate that the brochure about the post office spelt Macneill with a capital N, and wrongly identified a portrait of Aunt Mary Lawson as that of Grandmother Macneill.

Maud's birthplace, the little frame house at Clifton (New London) looking out over the incredibly blue water, has become an L. M. Montgomery museum. It has her wedding dress and shoes, and other souvenirs: in one of her scrapbooks this "relic hunter of the most aggravated description," as she once described herself, preserved a piece of fur from Daffy the cat. At Park Corner, by Anne's Lake of Shining Waters, home of Maud's Uncle John and Aunt Annie Campbell and her cousins, Stella, Frederica and George, can be seen the great wooden bed with its patchwork quilt where she slept in the upstairs bedroom; the parlour downstairs in which she was married, the organ that played for her wedding; first editions of her books; literary scrapbooks, photographs of her family, samples of her handmade lace and other treasures. On the stair landing, the small iron screw against which Maud measured her growth sticks out from the wall: just on a level with her nose "in the dawn of memory," level with her knees when she was grown up. The house, now the home of Ruth Campbell, widow of Uncle John Campbell's grandson James Townsend Campbell, is open to visitors, another L. M. Montgomery museum.

Prince Edward Island is honoured as the home of Canadian Confederation, the location of the conference held in Charlottetown in 1864 out of which came, eventually, the Canadian nation. But it would be hard to say whether this historic event has done more to bring fame to "the only Island there is" than the writing of L. M. Montgomery.

My debt to so many people who have helped me with information and reminiscences cannot be properly repaid. It is invidious to single out those who could give me more from those who, with less to contribute, nevertheless were unfailingly kind in providing what they could. Without any one of them, I could not have produced a work that I hope shows some insight and understanding, and contains as few as possible of the gaps and misinterpretations almost inevitable in any biography. The author must intrude in any work. I can only hope I have done justice to a complex and fascinating personality, with less to work from than I could have wished.

My heartfelt thanks, therefore, to all the following people and institutions for kind and willing assistance:

Chatelaine and its editor, Doris Anderson, for permission to use some sections of my article on L. M. Montgomery, and information collected in the course of research for it.

Archivists in Charlottetown, the Presbyterian Church of Canada, the Free Church of Scotland College, the United Church of Canada.

Dr F. W. P. Bolger, Chairman, Department of History, University of Prince Edward Island, for his encouraging interest in my work and his kind permission to quote from some of Miss Montgomery's youthful letters in *The Years Before "Anne."*

Mrs Ruth Campbell, of Park Corner, P.E.I., who received me privately in her home, now a museum in memory of L. M. Montgomery, where visitors may see the room in which she was married and some of the intimate souvenirs of her life. Mrs Campbell also gave kind permission to use several photographs in her possession.

John Gardner, formerly a reporter with the *Alloa Journal* and friend of George Boyd MacMillan, who brought Miss Montgomery's letters from Scotland for my use, and to whose wholehearted cooperation I owe much.

Professor Wilfrid Eggleston, who directed me to the unpublished correspondence with Ephraim Weber, and whose book *The Green Gables Letters* was an invaluable source.

Mrs Heber Jones (Charlottetown) who drove me to Cavendish; Mrs Murray Laird (Norval); and Miss Anita Webb (Toronto): three sisters whose childhood home was the house now known as Green Gables, and who, as relatives of Miss Montgomery, gave me many reminiscences and photographs.

Dr Stuart Macdonald, Toronto, L. M. Montgomery's son, who received me kindly, gave me information and documents about his famous mother, and his permission to quote from her letters.

George McMillan and his sister Margaretha, of Alloa, Scotland, to whom George Boyd MacMillan left his letters from L. M. Montgomery, and who gave me the unrestricted use of them, together with photographs and other information.

Miss Isobel Macneill, daughter of Maud Montgomery's cousin Murray, who provided family history and a family photograph.

James Kennedy Macneill of Boston, Maud's first cousin, whose childhood recollections have added much to this narrative, and whose friendship I value.

W. M'K. Murray, County Librarian of Clackmannan, whose initial response to my inquiry led to the discovery of the MacMillan letters.

Mrs. J. Goliath, librarian at Prince Albert, for information about that city.

Residents of Leaskdale and Norval, Ontario, whose reminiscences added much detail.

Mrs Donald St John, Uxbridge, Ontario, president of the Uxbridge Historical Society, who gathered together much information and many photographs, and made me familiar with the Leaskdale neighbourhood.

The Reverend and Mrs H. D. Smith who showed me the Norval Manse and Church.

Dr Moncrieff Williamson, director of the Confederation Art Gallery & Museum, Charlottetown, who holds the original manuscript of *Anne of Green Gables*, and who checked other information for me.

Public Archives of Canada and the National Library, Ottawa, whose staff was unfailingly obliging: especially Barbara Wilson (Manuscript Division) and Laura Adams (Newspaper Library).

Mollie Gillen

Toronto, Canada, and London, England, 1975

THE WHEEL OF THINGS

CHAPTER ONE

Beginnings

Wherever chance had brought this child to birth, she would have exulted in what her eyes beheld, made its beauties and eccentricities her own personal possessions, illumined her spirit with a passionate response to every experience, made every stick and stone, rock and tree, ditch and hillock in her environment part of an enchanted country to dwell in. "I had, in my imagination, a passport to fairyland," she wrote.

Had she been a waif in the Sahara Desert, the world would not have known Anne's Lake of Shining Waters, her Haunted Wood, her Green Gables, her Dryad's Bubble; would not have wandered the green corners and sun-steeped ferns of Emily's Land of Uprightness or seen the Wind Woman sweep over the hillside; would never have heard of Pat's Mince Pie Field or the Field of Farewell Summers. But a Maud Montgomery born by chance in the sandy wastes of Africa would still have been a child of secret delights, treasuring her Oasis of Rustling Palms, her Well of Echoes, her Shadowed Sandhills and the Caravans of Ancient Araby.

"The only Island there is," she would say, was her birthplace. In Clifton, a tiny community of green fields and rust-coloured roads on the Atlantic coast of Canada's smallest province, where the northern shore curves away to east and west, Hugh John Montgomery, a country merchant, and his young wife Clara became the parents of a daughter born on 30 November 1874—a date she would later remark with interest as the birth-date of another child, Winston Churchill. The little village of Clifton can't be found on today's maps of the Island. You must look instead for New London. Even then it won't be easy to find, its population little more than the few dozen families who lived in Clifton in 1874.

Hugh was nearly thirty-three, his bride not quite twenty-one when they had married the previous March. She had been Clara Woolner Macneill, daughter of Alexander and Lucy Woolner Macneill of Cavendish. The baby, named Lucy for her grandmother and Maud for herself, inherited a long line of Island ancestors from both father and mother, and some intriguing family legends of which she would make good use in later years. The Macneills and the Montgomerys had arrived in Prince Edward Island about the same time, and both families had produced figures of note in the community. Montgomerys, Macneills, Woolners, Townsends, Simpsons and Campbells still form a network of relationships across the Island, and this newest member of the clan carried some of the blood of all of them.

From Scotland came the first Montgomery in 1769, the first Macneill in 1770 or 1772: from England in 1775 the first Townsend, the first Woolner—comparative newcomer—in 1836. Family tradition says the first Montgomery—another Hugh John—had not intended to settle in Prince Edward Island. He had been heading for Quebec with his wife and family and two brothers. But when the ship anchored off the Island for water after the long Atlantic crossing, Hugh John's wife Mary MacShannon, who had been intolerably seasick, went ashore with the boat for a temporary escape, and made it permanent. Once on dry land, she firmly announced that nothing would ever make her embark again. All Hugh John's protests were in vain. He landed there, perforce, and established the family line in the New World. His grandson Donald, grandfather of the little Maud, was one of seventeen children: known as Big Donald to distinguish him from his cousin, Little Donald. Both became members of the Island Legislature: Big Donald, president of the Legislative Council from 1862, had been appointed to the Canadian Senate a year before this latest grandchild's birth, and served altogether fifty-four years as a legislator, twenty of them in the Senate.

The first Island Macneill, John, came from Campbelltown on the Kintyre Peninsula in the county of Argyll, bringing with him a romantic family history going back to the little

2

island of Colonsay in the Inner Hebrides. Coming unmarried, he settled in Charlottetown, capital of the province. Legend (again) has it that his log cabin was built where the present Legislative Building now stands, and that once, ordered by the governor to stop felling trees without permission, he felled the messenger as well and continued with his work. His marriage around 1780 brought Simpson blood into the family, and with his young wife Margaret he settled in Cavendish in 1791. Their eldest son William, born in Charlottetown in 1781 and great-grandfather of the young Maud Montgomery, had been a member of the Legislature from 1814 to 1834 and comes down in the family story as "Old Speaker Macneill." William was a man of substance: he owned the first four-wheeled carriage in Cavendish. He had been law clerk in Halifax, Nova Scotia, and shipbuilder at French River on the Island before he married, in 1806, Eliza Townsend, daughter of his partner and granddaughter of "a gentleman from England who had received from George Third . . . a grant of land for his services in the British Army." The Townsend tract was named Park Corner, from the name of the family estate in the land they had left. The gentleman's wife Elizabeth, so tradition has it, was so homesick that she stalked the floor of her new home for weeks still wearing her bonnet, refusing to remove it and demanding to return to England. Had she *slept* in it too, all that time, the little Maud used to wonder? There were forceful women in her family tree.

The small frame house in which Hugh and Clara Montgomery lived still stands, today painted white with green trim, but the store on the corner next door where Hugh John operated his business is now a gas station. The young man, possessed of an enterprising energy that would get him into a certain amount of trouble in later years, ambitiously traded with the West Indies and several American ports to further his interests in commerce and navigation. In 1875 he was appointed chairman of a commission to value lands mediating between the tenants and the government of Prince Edward Island, for which he was paid five dollars a day, but this work was completed a year later and his appointment terminated. Already he had started putting fingers in many pies.

This year—1876—brought sadness and a change in his life.

His young wife died from tuberculosis on September 14 in her parents' home at Cavendish when Maud was just over twenty-one months old.

Though she was a precocious child with a prodigious memory, and learned to read and write at an early age through a process of osmosis she could not understand or recall ("I might as well have been born with a capacity for reading"), it is hard to believe that so young a child could really remember seeing her mother lying dead in her coffin, as she later insisted. More likely the scene was conjured up in her vividly imaginative mind by the recollections of her elders. But she has given us a picture of the little girl in her embroidered white muslin dress, held in her weeping father's arms in the room where leaf-shadows danced on the floor, looking down on the fair hair, long lashes and thin face of her mother, so pretty and so still. After this, Maud lived in the old Macneill home in Cavendish with her maternal grandparents, Alexander and Lucy Macneill, and Hugh Montgomery took a variety of different occupations, including, it seems, connection with a firm shipping produce across the country.

It is possible that these widespread business dealings and his father's senatorial experience in a world beyond the small Island province awakened Hugh Montgomery's interest in the developing Canadian West. He also had friends who now lived in that part of Canada known as Saskatchewan, N.W.T. Until 1881, when his daughter was seven, it does not appear that he left Prince Edward Island for any extended period. For a couple of years prior to 1884 he spent summers in Prince Albert as agent for the Saskatchewan Forks Colonization Company, and worked in a real estate office, returning to the Island for the winters. Though she did not live with her father, Maud in these early years was not totally deprived of his presence. Indeed, many of her early recollections include her father's companionship and comments.

"I spent my childhood and girlhood in an old-fashioned Cavendish farmhouse, surrounded by apple orchards," she wrote. No place could have offered more to appease her insatiable appetite for beauty. Everything she has written is shot through with the memories of the child who ran free in the woods and meadows and sandhills of "the old north shore." Shafts of sunlight, shifting shadows, "the rich red of the winding roads . . . the dark dappling of spruce and fir . . . the bracing tang of the salt air"—these were to become her refuge and her inspiration. "Everything was invested with a kind of fairy grace and charm, emanating from my own fancy, the trees that whispered nightly around the old house where I slept, the woodsy nooks I explored, the homestead fields, each individualized by some oddity or fence or shape, the sea whose murmur was never out of my ears—all were radiant with 'the glory and the dream' . . . amid all the commonplaces of life, I was very near to a kingdom of ideal beauty. Between it and me hung only a thin veil. I could never draw it quite aside, but sometimes a wind fluttered it and I caught a glimpse of the enchanting realm beyond—only a glimpse—but those glimpses have always made life worth while."

This would be the "flash" that pulled Emily of New Moon into ecstasy. This instant response to beauty would stay with Maud Montgomery throughout her sixty-seven years of life— the shiver of sudden recognition, the soul-healing touch of splendour. In her mid-fifties she wrote to a friend: "Coming home from a sick call I saw something that suddenly rested me—the pines on the western hill dark against a sunset sky. Oh, there was the way, the truth, the light—sheer ecstasy above the world possessed me—re-youthed me. . . ."

Always, the richness of her inner life—the joys she found in nature, in words, in friendships—would support her through the buffetings of fortune. But there was a core of steel in Maud Montgomery that went beyond even this: the sense of duty. It would delay her marriage until she was thirty-six while she stayed to help an aging grandmother, hold her rigidly in the role of minister's wife as she saw it, and strengthen her in a continuing struggle with her husband's melancholia. It also did much to cancel out the gift for happiness with which she had been born: at one and the same time making disappointments easier to cope with and harder to bear.

It is said that she was a solitary child, though she was surrounded by relatives, uncles, aunts, cousins living not too far away. Her grandfather Montgomery was one of seventeen

5

children, her grandfather Macneill one of eleven, her father one of eleven, her mother one of six. Grandfather Macneill, as well as farmer, was also the Cavendish postmaster, which meant many people coming and going from the house. Moreover, the school was just across the road, with children straggling in and out and shouting in the playground. It was less loneliness than delicious fantasy that provided the little girl with two companions to chatter to, looking-glass figures who came to shadowy life in the oval glass doors of the bookcase used as a china cabinet. In the left-hand door was Katie Maurice, a child of Maud's own age, with whom she shared endless confidences. Behind the right-hand door lived Lucy Gray, a grown-up widowed lady who entrusted Maud with sad tales of past tragedies. Katie Maurice and Lucy Gray did not like each other, and Maud favoured Katie, but she was polite to Lucy Gray and conscientious about including both in her friendship and attention.

If solitary, Maud was never truly a lonely child, except perhaps in her very earliest years; not with the intense, passionate inner life she lived, with her eager curiosity and effortless imagination. Trees—particularly trees—leaves, shadows, flowers, clouds, kittens—especially kittens—sea-shells and sea-spray, moonlight and sunshine, all were the breath of life to the young Maud.

CHAPTER TWO

*Passport
to fairyland*

Though her treasured memories were not etched with the singular clarity of nostalgia until after infancy—"the first six years of my life are hazy in recollection"—isolated memories rear up, monoliths of terror, of fascination, of humiliation, of new understandings. At four, she was comforted by discovering "the exact location of Heaven": not remote and unattainable beyond the farthest star, but in the attic of the Clifton Presbyterian Church. Heaven could be reached through a square hole in the ceiling—Maud's unmarried Aunt Emily herself had pointed upward silently in response to a whispered query. Why, then, did they not sometimes go up to visit Mother, wondered Maud?

She was nine years old before she first learned the reality of sorrow and mental suffering, watching her kitten Pussy-willow dying from poison. But four years earlier, on a visit to Grandfather Montgomery's farm at Park Corner, she had gained firsthand knowledge of physical pain. She learned the hard way, by picking up the wrong end of a red-hot poker. Though she spent a miserable night of real suffering, her arm up to the elbow in a pail of ice-water, one corner of her mind enjoyed the ensuing commotion. "For the time being, I was splendidly, satisfyingly important." She became more important over the next few days, when the violent headache that developed was diagnosed as typhoid fever. Excitement caused by the arrival of Grandmother Macneill, summoned in a hurry, raised the small patient's temperature so alarmingly that her worried father hastily informed her that Grandma had gone home again. Believing his attempt to soothe her, the child refused to recognize her grandmother during subsequent days of delirium, insisting that she must be an unpopular Mrs Murphy "who was tall and thin, like Grandmother." When recognition returned, she could hardly bear to be out of her grandmother's arms in case she disappeared again.

At five, too, Maud knew with awful certainty that the world would end next Sunday, having overhead an item read aloud from the newspaper. It *must* be true—"it had been *printed*." In an agony of wretchedness she awaited the Last Trump and the Day of Judgment, unable to comprehend the casual and unheeding routine activities of her elders under threat of such enormous doom. Until that interminable Sunday ended and "the beautiful green world of blossom and sunshine" proved to be still intact, she cowered in mortal terror. Two chapters in *The Story Girl* would recreate that terror for the children in Maud's 1910 novel.

Visits to Uncle John and Aunt Annie Campbell, and to Grandfather Montgomery, both at Park Corner—their farms almost facing one another across the road—were infrequent but cherished occasions. The drive to get there was "such a pretty one, those winding thirteen miles through hill and wood, and by river and shore." But two of the rivers had to be crossed by "drawbridges," and Maud was afraid of them. It was a fear that persisted throughout her life. Did that all-too-vivid imagination picture the bridge rising up and depositing them, carriage, horses and all, in a heap on the road below?

Uncle John Campbell's house was "a big white one, smothered in orchards," standing above the Lake of Shining Waters, with a pantry full of goodies to be raided in later days with three boisterous cousins. Grandfather Montgomery's home was a charming old frame house "full of cupboards and nooks, and little, unexpected flights of stairs." Maud dearly loved the pair of white, green-spotted china dogs that stood on the sitting room mantel and which, her father told her with great solemnity, leaped down to the hearth and barked when they heard the strokes of midnight. She was never allowed to satisfy her ardent longing to stay up late enough to catch them at this magic; and insult was added to injury when it was revealed that the story was not, in fact, true. Father had actually *lied* to her. But he saved his reputation by explaining that the dogs had to *hear* the clock strike. And of course, china dogs could not hear.

If visits to Park Corner were infrequent, visits to town were even more rare. Five-year-old Maud's first taste of this heady excitement brought a small adventure. Town was a place of exotic delights—shop-window displays, an abundance of nuts and candies and oranges, and streets full of glamorous strangers. Never afraid to venture (except in the face of ghoulies and ghosties and other powers of darkness), Maud slipped confidently down a side street, absorbing amazing new experiences while her grandparents chatted on a corner with friends. A woman was shaking rugs *"on the top of a house.* I felt dizzy with excitement over such a topsy-turvy sight. *We* shook rugs in the yard."

A dim room full of barrels and curly wood-shavings rewarded a daring descent of steps through an open door. And then, on the way back to guardians who had not yet missed her, Maud met a kindred spirit—a black-eyed, black-haired little girl carrying a pitcher. "We told each other how old we were, and how many dolls we had, and almost everything else there was to tell except our names which neither of us thought about. When we parted, I felt as though I were leaving a life long friend."

So friendly and outgoing a child would not have failed, when similar chance offered to make contact, however brief and superficial, with any child coming to the post office, or wandering by the farm, or (before her own school days) going to and from school in the "white-washed, low-eaved building on the side of the road just outside our gate" next to a spruce grove that was Maud's idea of fairyland. In the summer of 1881, when she was six, Aunt Emily took her to the schoolhouse, neatly and respectably shod with the buttoned boots she so much resented in the company of barefoot fellow pupils. She felt discrimination in other ways, too. Children from more distant homes could stay for a delightful schoolyard lunch, sitting in sociable groups under playground trees, their bottles of milk cooled from a morning stashed in one of the hidey-holes in the brook that bubbled through the grounds. Deprived Maud, except on a few welcome stormy days, had to go home for a hot midday dinner. Later, mortification and teasing had to be endured with the wearing of "baby" pinafores, detestable long sack-like garments with the sleeves that no other child wore.

School discipline was harsh at times. Maud remembered in furious italics a *whipping* the teacher administered to impress on her the iniquity of using the phrase *by the skin of my teeth.* "He said it was slang. If I had but known then what I know now!!!" she wrote some twenty-five years later, the memory still rankling. "It is in *Job.*" But it was her experience of just this kind of incident that would bring her child characters leaping from the page in suppressed fury, smarting over similar injustices.

For gregarious Maud, however, school was not on the whole an unpleasurable experience, and she had the delight, the following summer, of acquiring two young companions, Wellington and David Nelson (Well and Dave), who came to board with the Macneills for school attendance.

Her friendship with these youngsters, and her spontaneous chatter to the small stranger in Charlottetown are a little at variance with some of her later recollections. "I was a lonely child," she would write some twenty-three years after, but by this she meant that in her very earliest years she had few intimate playmates, and in her adolescence she lacked the freedom her contemporaries enjoyed. "I was shut out from all social life, even such as this small country settlement could offer, debarred from the companionship of other children, and in early youth, other young people. I had no companionship except that of books and solitary rambles in wood and fields. This drove me in on myself and early forced me to construct for myself a world of fancy and imagination very different indeed from the world in which I lived." Yet her own account of these pre-teen years, in *The Alpine Path*, published in 1917, is sharp and clear, filled with the childhood joys that ring so true in her books. In retrospect, a natural shyness and reserve and the lack of child companions in her home may have led her to overemphasize her solitary state, interpreting the richness of her inner life at that time as a greater loneliness than she actually experienced. And it is possible that awareness of her father's seeming desertion grew in his daughter's mind into a memory of a childhood more lonely than the reality.

The three children ran riot in field and wood and sand-dunes, Maud with her long hair flying: gathered flowers, picked berries, fished the brooks in the woods for trout (Maud managed—shudderingly—to put her own worm on the hook, and earned the boys' respect by catching a large fish on one memorable occasion); laced together a playhouse from fir boughs in a circle of young spruce trees to the west of the Macneill front orchard; planted little gardens, where the ever-green rock plant *live-forever* overran carrots, lettuces, phlox, sweet peas, and beans that "persisted in coming up with their skins over their heads," promptly (and ruinously) pulled off by the young gardeners; carried eight o'clock breakfasts, mid-day dinners and often suppers to the fishing house on the shore for hungry French-Canadian mackerel fishers who had gone out in Grandfather Macneill's boat at three or four on sum-mer mornings; scrambled among pools and rocks for shells and pebbles and mussels, gathering up the "great, white, empty 'snail' shells, as big as our fists, that had been washed ashore from some distant strand or deep sea haunt"; ate dulse "by the yard," perched on rocks carved in queer shapes by con-stantly crashing Atlantic waves; chased each other, tumbling and shouting, through fragrant fields of new-cut hay; revelled in the trees individually named by Maud—apple trees in both orchards known as Aunt Emily's tree, Uncle Leander's tree, Little Syrup tree, Spotty tree, the Spider tree, the slim White Lady birch in a corner of the front orchard, and the spruce and maple so closely intertwined that they could only be The Lovers.

Both Well and Dave had a store of ghost stories. In summer twilight, companionably perched on the back porch steps, Well told tales that curdled young blood with delicious, half-believed terror, conjuring up a grandfather whose wraith had been seen tending the cows while his real body lay sleeping on the sofa; envisioning a terrible, headless "lamb of fire" pursu-ing unwary evil-doers in the dark; and so realistically peopling the Haunted Wood with "white things" fluttering in the small hours that an all-too-real "white thing" flapping one evening under the juniper tree sent the three children shrieking from their field-play for the house. Grandmother, who should have been quietly sewing in her room, wasn't. The three tore off for aid and comfort to a neighbour's, where derision greeted their horrified burblings. But no, they stammered, it wasn't the white calf they had tried at first to tell themselves it was. No, it wasn't queer Mag Laird, wandering vacantly along the lanes. It was a ghost, dreadfully advancing to punish sinful children. Sceptical servants equipped with pail of oats and pitchfork, returned to report no calf, no spectral visitor ("This did not surprise us. Of course [it] would vanish when it had fulfilled its mission"). Only Grandfather, disgustedly calling to collect the trembling trio, was able to reassure them. The "white thing" had been a tablecloth, set out on the grass to bleach in the sun, and dropped by Grandmother, who had sallied forth, knitting in hand, to retrieve it; and, bending down to pick up a ball of wool fallen into the dyke, was not visible to the children.

CHAPTER THREE

Young
writer

Aunt Mary Lawson, a beloved great-aunt, youngest of Speaker Macneill's eleven children, to whose vivid story-telling about her own youth, her ancestors, and the activities of pioneer days Maud would owe many of the anecdotes in her books, wrote some years later to a nephew about their forebears. "[They] filled a large space in the moral, intellectual, and religious development of the country, and . . . were strongly impressed with the idea that they were above the common herd." Island records are full of family names among the magistrates, teachers, ministers and legistators of the province. With that heritage, Maud grew up with a strong and well-justified pride of family.

Her grandfather, Alexander Macneill, she described as "a man of strong and pure literary tastes, with a considerable knack of prose composition." Lucy Woolner, his wife, born at Dunwich in Suffolk and educated in England before coming to Canada at the age of twelve, was accounted a remarkable woman by all who knew her. A much younger grandchild, the youngest son of Maud's Uncle Leander by his third wife, who spent pre-teen summers in Cavendish in the last ten years of Lucy Macneill's almost eighty-seven-year life, still speaks of her with love and admiration. "Grandmother was one of the most lovable, thoughtful, competent, and unselfish women I ever had the privilege of knowing. To her last days in 1911 she ran the home, the post office, our own family on our visits each summer, and she utterly spoiled me with her attentions and kindnesses. She was surely an unforgettable lady and strong too, as I recall seeing her walking back from the well with two buckets of water when well into her eighties."

It is possible that the youthful Ken Macneill, some twenty-five years younger than his famous cousin, saw a softer, more outgoing grandmother than Maud did during her growing years, at a time when religious practices and principles were even narrower and stricter, and social attitudes still more restrictive. The total responsibility for rearing and training a child does not always allow the "spoiling" indulged in when the child's training is known to be in other, and competent, hands. The child Maud dearly loved many aspects of her grandmother; but there are hints in letters from the adult Maud that resentment and rebellion against a rigidity in her upbringing went deep, and left a residue of bitterness. "In material respects [my grandparents] were good and kind to me and I am sincerely grateful to them, but in many respects they were unwise in their treatment of me."

Aspects of Lucy Woolner Macneill come to life in Anne's guardian Marilla Cuthbert and Emily's Aunt Elizabeth Murray, strong women endowed with human character weaknesses they may recognize and deplore but be powerless to change; women stern but just, governed by a sense of duty, slightly tyrannical, not dour but not outgoing, capable of more affection than they can allow themselves to show, seldom uncertain of the principles by which they lived.

Maud's heroines often suffer under the same kind of humiliations and frustrations as she resented, and reflect her own feelings of outrage when forced into similar situations by well-meaning adults. She writes of her "anger, humiliation and disgust" when, after discovery of some childish naughtiness, she was forced by her grandmother to kneel on the floor and pray to God to be forgiven for being such a bad girl. Grandmother "meant well," but could never have pictured the impotent anger and "queer sense of degradation" the child was feeling at what was an invasion of personal privacy and dignity. Certainly she could never have realized the hatred and disgust for prayer and religion—"what *she* called prayer and religion"—Maud would carry into her adult life.

"Something inside me was outraged. . . . To force a human

soul to utter words of prayer and contrition when not in a fit state to do so—when stormy rebellion and bitterness filled it!"

The result was a hangover of humiliation that "manifests itself in a *feeling* which lurks under all the beliefs and conclusions of my reason—that religion and all connected with it was something which—like sex—it is necessary to have but made one feel ashamed for all that."

This rebellion against religion as it was manifest to the imaginative little girl growing up in a strict Presbyterian home was fostered by a twice-a-year visit from a Bible Society traveller, a thin, pale man with a straggly beard and squeaky voice. Hunched over a fire on a frosty night, he suddenly asked: "Little girl, isn't it nice to be a Christian?" He would have been appalled if he had been a mind-reader. If *he* was, *she* certainly didn't want to be. Remembering his "shivery, bony form, pinched blue face, purple hands," Maud was never able totally to separate the two ideas "so incongruously wedded at that fatal moment." How difficult this would make her future role as minister's wife she has intimated in later letters to friends.

Two events when she was seven shook her world. In the winter of 1881-82 her Aunt Emily was married to John Montgomery in a whirl of pre-wedding baking, cake-frosting, visiting relatives, and a night of gala supper, dancing and games after the seven o'clock ceremony. For the first time, Maud was allowed to stay up past midnight—probably for lack of a room not occupied with festivities. When departure time came, the bridegroom who was carrying off her beloved Aunt Emily found himself assaulted verbally and physically by a small fury weeping with weariness and sick enough from over-indulgence in the goodies to be laid up for a week afterwards.

And in the spring, her father went off to Saskatchewan on probably the first of the trips that ended with his permanent residence there. Maud's various child heroines were often given the same fatherless status. Emily of New Moon, in particular, is shown as having had a close relationship with the father she lost to death, and clearly was bereft by the loss. Maud, living in another house and therefore not as close to him in everyday living, probably did not miss her father as much as she might have done: nevertheless, his absence from her life for increasingly long periods seems to have left a gap.

For all its quiet, backwater atmosphere, the Macneill home was a cultured and literate environment. Not many books stood on the shelves, but the child devoured them all. Hans Andersen's *Tales* led to an entracing dream-world. A two-volume *History of the World*, full of coloured pictures, covered time from Adam and Eve to Queen Victoria. There were poets—Tennyson, Whittier, Scott, Longfellow, Byron, Milton, Burns. A few novels—*Rob Roy, The Pickwick Papers* and Lord Lytton's *Zanoni*: these, though, with the poets, were banned Sunday reading. For Sundays, allowable books were one about Pacific Islands missionaries "in which I revelled because it was full of pictures of cannibal chiefs with the most extraordinary hair arrangements"; *The Pilgrim's Progress*— "read and re-read with never-failing delight": and Talmage's *Sermons*, not so much for its religion—"though at that age I liked the Talmage brand much"—but for its anecdotes and lively word-pictures. "His sermons were as interesting as fiction." In later years, Maud would shudder away from Talmage.

Top favourite Sunday reading, however, was a small volume entitled *The Memoir of Anzonetta Peters*, the story of a saintly child of ten, who died after five years of agonizing and uncomplaining illness and who talked in Scripture instead of English. Anzonetta was transferred bodily to *Emily of New Moon*, the most autobiographical of Maud Montgomery's books. The child Maud identified with Anzonetta, envying her the very obvious admiration of her biographer and the central position she occupied on her little stage—a position Maud herself always enjoyed holding, both then and later. Besides, tragedy (in fiction anyway) was so emotionally satisfying. After feasting her eyes on glamour in the fashion pages of *Godey's Lady's Book*, to which her grandmother subscribed, Maud wept piteously and happily over the sufferings of the unselfish and peerlessly lovely heroines in the fiction pages.

Until February 1886, when Maud was eleven and the newly

founded Cavendish Literary Society set up an embryo library, her reading material was probably confined to what could be found in home and school. But it was enough. It was only a step from reading stories to writing them: and one can only wish for some Time Machine to whisk into today the biographies of cats and dolls, histories of visits, descriptions of favourite haunts, and critical reviews of books that were produced by the young author in the "stacks of manuscripts, long ago reduced to ashes."

Maud was nine, she says, when she made her first attempt at writing poetry, inspired by "a little black, curly-covered atrociously printed copy" of James Thomson's *The Seasons*. Paper on which to write would have been hard to come by except for the lucky chance of the long red post-office "letter-bills," written on one side only and discarded three times a week by her grandfather the postmaster. On one of these she penned the pretentious, clearly derivative little poem called *Autumn*, beginning:

"Now autumn comes, laden with peach and pear;
The sportsman's horn is heard throughout the land,
And the poor partridge, fluttering, falls dead."

Even from the beginning, Maud could scan. She was able to present this masterpiece to her father, home for a while from the West. It didn't, he remarked, sound much like poetry.

" 'It's blank verse,' I cried.
'Very blank,' said father."

The poetry phase now invaded the classroom, when sums and spelling should have been scribbled on slates. Maud and Alma, a friend with her own flair for poetry, busily scribbled poems instead: first addressed to each other, then developed as a daring series of verses on various teachers. The current teacher, noticing their absorption and quite rightly feeling it could not be inspired by sums, swept the slates out of their hands. The horrified poets, cowering before the expected on-slaught, were spared the ordeal of hearing their verses sarcastically read aloud (as Emily of New Moon was not); but the verses were rubbed off with frenzied haste when the slates

17

were returned. Maud would turn such incidents to good account, embroidering them and enlarging their effect, in her books.

At twelve, she had no way of judging the quality of her verse, afraid to hand the poems over to possible laughter and scorn. An opportunity to earn an impartial judgment occurred during the visit of a lady with a reputation as a singer. Had the lady ever heard of a song called *Evening Dreams,* Maud asked, quaking? The lady thought she might know, if she could hear the words. Two verses of Maud's current masterpiece were stammered out by the now petrified poetess: the lady said she did not know them, but that they were "very pretty."

This, her first commendation, sent Maud dancing in ecstasy through the birches. The poem might even be good enough for publication. She copied it carefully that winter and sent it off, first to an American publication whence it speedily returned, and then, after this first rejection had cooled her enthusiasm for a full year, to the Charlottetown *Examiner,* with no better luck. These first rejections dashed her hopes but not her need to write. The stacks of manuscripts grew: more poems and, by now, stories too, usually full of tragedy and tribulation, "in which almost everyone died." The Story Club in *The Story Girl* came from a real-life incident, when she and two school friends wrote a story from the same plot—"a very tragic plot . . . the heroines were all drowned while bathing on Cavendish sandshore." A first-person story followed, entitled *My Graves:* the harrowing journey of a Methodist minister's wife from circuit to circuit across Canada, leaving a child buried at each stop from Newfoundland to Vancouver.

The chrysalis author was struggling toward what she fondly hoped would be butterfly wings.

CHAPTER FOUR

The
Marco Polo

Some of the early disappointments of the young writer in the *Emily* books, whose work failed to win in school competitions, probably mirror fifteen-year-old Maud's firsthand experience when her account of *The Wreck of the Marco Polo* was placed only third for Queens County in the Canada Prize Competition of 1890. That the second place went to another Cavendish school pupil would have added salt to the wound. The account by "Miss Lucy," said the Charlottetown *Patriot* of May 31, "is a very chaste description of a sad event of coast life."

Miss Lucy had been only eight in the summer of 1883 when, at nine o'clock on the morning of Wednesday, July 25, a tremendous sight brought all the residents of Cavendish flying to the shore. They saw the famous old ship "coming straight on before the northern gale with every stitch of canvas set. She grounded about three hundred yards from the shore and as she struck the crew cut the rigging, and the huge masts went over with a crash that was heard for a mile, above the roaring of the storm."

The 1,625-ton, three-decker *Marco Polo* had been famous in her day. Built at Saint John, New Brunswick, in 1851, she had had a distinguished career for ten years as a modified clipper on the Liverpool-Australia run. After an unhappy launching into a spring tide, when she ended up jammed in the mud on the far side of the creek and eventually capsized in the ebbing tide, she was dug out, refloated, and sent to Liverpool with a cargo of timber. Bought for the Black Ball Line of Australian packets, extensively and luxuriously refitted to take passengers, she made a record outward run of sixty-eight days and a record round trip of five months twenty-one days on her maiden voyage under Captain James Nicol ("Bully") Forbes: on her return to the Mersey she was hung with a banner reading THE FASTEST SHIP IN THE WORLD.

Under other captains, she maintained her reputation until 1861, when she hit an iceberg on the homeward run and had to limp to Valparaiso for repairs. By 1867 she had become a tramp, ending up under the Norwegian flag. Her last voyage, under Captain A. P. Bull of Christiania, had started from Quebec on July 19, 1883, with a load of pine deals and ends.

There are divided opinions about the reason for the wreck of the ship (phonetically metamorphosed by one paper into *Mark Apollo*). The first version implied fraud: that the vessel, creaking and now unprofitable, was deliberately wrecked for the insurance. The second—that she was the victim of a gale in the Gulf of St Lawrence and, leaking so badly that the pumps could not cope, was driven on shore to prevent her foundering—had Maud's personal endorsement. In the margin of a volume belonging to one of her relatives—an account of the square-rigged merchant marine of British North America, *Wooden Ships and Iron Men*—she has written firmly, "purposely run on shore to save crew & cargo as she had started an unstoppable leak."

It has been claimed that no bad weather was reported in the gulf at the time of the wreck. However, Maud herself was a witness, and even though she was only eight, a very observant one. Moreover, the report of the wreck in the official government sessional paper states, under the heading of "Statement of Wrecks and Casualties to Sea-going Vessels," that the stranding was "due to thick weather."

The unforgettable sight of the great trapped ship, smothered in Atlantic spray, photographed itself indelibly on the impressionable young mind as the little girl watched spellbound from the red sands of the Cavendish beach; or perhaps, for better viewing, from the red rocks twenty to thirty feet high. It had been rumoured at first that two lady passengers had shared the crew's hazardous adventure, but this was contradicted by the captain, who wrote to the *Patriot* from Rankin House Hotel in Charlottetown. "There were no lady or gentleman passengers on board the ship, therefore no lady or gentlemen passengers were in peril."

The arrival on shore next day of the twenty crew members —a motley, colourful lot, Irish, English, Scots, Spaniards, Swedes, Dutch, German and two Tahitians, who boarded out among Cavendish farmhouses while investigation into the wreck continued—gave even more impact to the event. For weeks the men roared through the quiet countryside in truck-wagons, shouting and singing. The two Tahitians, with "woolly heads, thick lips, and gold earrings" not too far removed from the pictures in the missionary book, were an especial joy to Maud. Important people from town, too, came and went, standing on the beach to look at the stranded ship: the Norwegian vice-consul, insurance men, surveyors. On August 1 a Wreck Sale was advertised "For the Benefit of all Concerned." The Hull and Materials of the Barque *Marco Polo*, plus the cargo, would be put up to auction where she lay stranded, at noon on the 8th.

On the day of the sale—a fine, clear day—Cavendish was crowded with buyers—"every town, village and hamlet from Alberton to Georgetown was represented." Others came from as far away as Quebec, Saint John, Sackville, Moncton, Shediac and Kouchibouguac in New Brunswick.

The little girl's darting eyes would have missed no detail of the solemn, important businessmen in city clothes, with gold watch chains, who stared, squint-eyed and appraising, at the rock-fast vessel, nodding their approval or their doubts to each other and oblivious of the *chiel amang them takin' notes*. How many of them turned up later as Lofty John, the Awkward Man, Jarback Priest, Drowned John Penhallow, drawn in bold brushstrokes on the pages of Maud's books? And did she think about her great-great-grandfather John Macneill and her great-great-great-grandfather William Simpson, both of whom had arrived on the Island from shipwrecked vessels?

There was a bustle that day in the Macneill home, where the auctioneer from Charlottetown—another Alexander Macneill—brought in a total of about eight thousand dollars. The stores and fittings were sold in small lots, "many being seem-ingly anxious to own something which belonged to the great packet ship." It is possible that even today there are people in Prince Edward Island who will tell you—as people were telling visitors up to forty years ago—that the great explorer Marco Polo actually landed at Cavendish Capes.

The Norwegian captain boarded at the Macneill home, his excellent but sometimes confused English—"Thank you for your kindness *against* me, little Miss Maud"—delighting the child's quick ear for eccentricities. When the crew was paid off, all the men sitting on the Macneill lawn beneath the parlour window and feeding biscuits to old dog Gyp, the three children saw, goggle-eyed, the table top vanish beneath an unimagined wealth of gold sovereigns.

On a cool summer night some forty-five years later Maud would stand on Cavendish beach and bring to vivid life the story of the wreck for a group of young people gathered around a bonfire on the sand. "She made us see it before our very eyes," one of them has recalled.

The small schoolhouse provided the growing girl with an excellent basic education, extended by her own avid curiosity and her literary and cultural family heritage. The Charlotte-town *Patriot* of Friday, July 4, 1890, reported the regular half-yearly examinations held a week earlier at the Cavendish school "in the presence of the trustees and parents of the chil-dren. Classes were examined in Reading, English Grammar and Analysis, English History, Geography, Arithmetic and Geometry. The examination extended over three hours and was very thorough and minute in the different branches. The pupils showed good progress and creditable proficiency in all the subjects upon which they were examined."

On the following Monday, an "entertainment" was given by the scholars in Cavendish Hall, consisting of thirty-nine items, in five of which Miss Maud Montgomery was indi-vidually named: she could also have been in eight others—those performed by "the choir," or "eight girls," or "school." Her personal contributions consisted of instrumental music —*Swedish Wedding March* and a *Medley*; a "reading speech" entitled *Buckwood's Wedding*, which she performed with Master Garfield Stewart: and two recitations, *Over the Hills to the Poor House* and *The Schoolmaster's Guests*. "The above lengthy and varied programme," said the *Patriot* benevolently, "was rendered with great spirit and success by the scholars. All, from the youngest to the oldest acquitted themselves to the satisfaction and delight of the audience. . . . The unanimous verdict of the audience was that a more enjoyable evening had not been spent for a long time."

Elusive pictures of Maud on this night flash into the mind with each mention of her name in the *Patriot's* columns—the small, intense fifteen-year-old, delicate of feature and graceful in person as she would always be, eyes shining with excitement; with the determination to excel that informed her every act; proud of achievement; her secret heart impatient for the future in which she intended to succeed; and—surely —proud of the satisfaction that she would see in the faces of the grandparents who had brought thus far the child of their dead daughter.

But the shine in Maud's eyes on the night of the "entertainment" covered a greater excitement still—the knowledge that she was about to embark on an almost transcontinental journney. She was going to Prince Albert, Saskatchewan, N.W.T., with Grandfather Senator Montgomery, to stay with her father, who had remarried in April 1887 and could now offer a home to his daughter.

CHAPTER FIVE

A very active and energetic man

Hugh Montgomery, with his keen business sense, had been quick to see Prince Albert's potential. The *Saskatchewan Herald* at Battleford had been publishing articles for some years about the community: in February 1880 a Prince Albert correspondent had glowed with pride over its rapid expansion.

"This settlement is making rapid progress . . . we have had a good steam-mill for some time . . . it is reported . . . that two new grist-mills are to be built here during the coming summer. . . . We are living in the expectation of seeing some more branches of business and trade spring up. . . . We very much want a watchmaker, shoemaker, tanner, soap factory, baker, butcher, tailor, painter, a furrier—who might be a merchant or a tailor at the same time; and a goodly number of common laborers could find constant employment. . . . Our settlement is not nearly filled up yet. We have room for hundreds, yes, thousands of energetic men, women and children, but not one square inch for a dead beat. . . ."

In 1880, travel was still not without difficulties in the area. "Some of our best citizens are contemplating a journey to the capital, to advance the interests of the place. They intend going by the river with dogs. A number of our merchants are making ready to perform the same journey overland. . . ."

In November 1882 (its first number) the Prince Albert *Times* had reported that "Hugh J. Montgomery Esq., of Saskatchewan Forks Colonization Co., who has been engaged during the summer in locating the lands of the Company in the neighborhood of the Forks, has taken up his winter quarters in Prince Albert, after having made a general examination of the Company's tract." The lively development of the area had continued: the paper remarked on the improvement in lighting in the new Presbyterian church by the addition of new chandeliers, on meetings of the Saskatchewan Curling Club, on hopes for a mail service to begin shortly; and asked why some enterprising person didn't build a large hall for concerts and balls, with dressing rooms.

Montgomery seems to have shuttled back and forth between east and west on many occasions and in all seasons. In mid-January it was noted that "Mr Montgomery, who has been a resident of Prince Albert for the last six months, goes east in a few days, as far as Toronto and Ottawa, on a visit to friends. The many friends he has made during his stay here wish him *bon voyage*, and a speedy return to Prince Albert, where he intends to reside for some time to come." He returned on April 10, and on the 18th was advertising from his office at Tait & Co.'s Block, above Ashdown's Store, in two and a half column inches, as a Real Estate Agent, Auctioneer, Etc.; Money invested, Best of Representation given, A number of very desirable town lots and farm lands for sale ("We wish him success," the *Times* editorialized).

By May, reported as having disposed of over two-thousand-dollars-worth of property in the previous week, and adding to his repertoire the provision of patents where required, he was well integrated into the social life of the community. For the Queen's birthday, he was a judge at the programme of sports, amusements and pony races. In July the paper was regretting the severe illness that had caused him to be "confined to his Quarters for the past week," and hoped soon to see him "enjoying his usual good health and spirits." Later that month he moved his office into McLean & Elliott's law chambers.

In August he sold a lot for the construction of a new Methodist church in the fall. Prince Albert, said the *Times*, was now a favourite summer resort: all the hotels were overcrowded, and by October the proprietors were planning a business directory to list the many enterprises that had sprung up in a steadily more prosperous community.

On 1 May 1884, Montgomery was appointed to the Department of the Interior as a forest ranger based at the Crown Timber Office in Prince Albert, with an annual salary of seven hundred dollars plus twenty per cent of dues on timber seized. Having been given the job while he was at Winnipeg, and having had the intention, he said, of returning to Prince Edward Island had he not received it, he protested a departmental veto on reimbursement of his expenses from Winnipeg to Prince Albert. These totalled $87.95, covering hotel at Winnipeg while awaiting instructions, train fare to "Capelle" and overnight hotel bill, stage fare thence to Prince Albert, meals en route (seven days) and cartage and freight on luggage. The claim had been disallowed on the grounds that he was already a resident of the West. His father, the Senator, brought big guns to bear in a July letter to the Acting Minister of the Interior. Hugh John received his money.

A year later he came under fire from his supervisor, the Crown Timber Agent David Waggoner, who strongly objected to his taking private commissions while being paid as a government official. Hugh Montgomery, with his usual ambition and keen eye for opportunities, had been doing some moonlighting and, continuing unrepentant, was soon embroiled in some public bitterness that found him defendant at an official inquiry into his conduct in mid-October 1885. Waggoner, whose distress over his activities had increased, had written to the Deputy Minister of the Interior in September enclosing a published letter of accusation against his forest ranger, which accusation he felt compelled to endorse. Among other things, the writer accused Montgomery—"This horse jobber, land speculator, conveyancer, land agent, would-be town assessor . . . [and] store agent for Hudson's Bay Co's blankets and other goods"—of publicly belittling Waggoner.

Montgomery was suspended, and at the inquiry held before Homestead Inspector R. S. Park, prosecution and defence witnesses were heard. Charges of fraudulent dealings in land and diseased horses were ramblingly presented by one claimant, whose honesty seems to have been pretty well discredited by defence witnesses. This, and private inquiries by Mr Park, led to little more than censure for Montgomery—"a very active and energetic man," wrote Mr Park, "[who] would take hold of any business that came in his way, so it is quite possible, if there was not much to do in the Crown timber office, that Mr Montgomery employed himself in making an addition to his salary . . . [but] he should be severely censured in making remarks against his superior officer calculated to destroy his influence. . . . This disagreement . . . has done a good deal towards augmenting the feelings against government officials."

It was true, said Mr Park, that some citizens probably resented a man on government salary competing with private individuals. However, "I should be sorry to see Mr Montgomery suffer for his indiscretion." Park recommended removal to serve under another officer.

The Dominion Lands Office agreed. "The extreme penalty of dismissal would not be imposed, but . . . he should be severely reprimanded, warned against a repetition of the offence, and reinstated."

His reinstatement took Hugh Montgomery to Battleford, switching places with the ranger already there, and with instructions to work under the agent of Dominion Lands: and—perhaps to keep the idle hands of this volatile civil servant from further mischief—"to assist in the office generally when not engaged upon work connected with timber matters." By March 1886 he was writing, somewhat tongue-in-cheek, to the "Hon. Minister of Interior, Ottawa," suggesting modestly that his good behaviour on forest-ranger duties pushed into overtime by his dutiful daytime attention to Land Agent office work surely deserved some recognition in increased salary.

He may already at this time have been considering the marriage with his second wife, Mary Ann McRae, which would take place a year later. But by October, when he was back in Prince Albert for a while, he fell foul of Waggoner's principles again. Waggoner was after him at once, writing more in sorrow than in anger to the Commissioner in Winnipeg about his conduct.

Irrepressible and canny Hugh was up to his old tricks again. Opportunities in this burgeoning community were too good for him to miss. Montgomery had had the temerity to be first to operate as soon as the issuing of scrip began and "broke the rules in consequence of his over anxiety to make money." Montgomery had in some way defrauded two poor men over the sale of land at the forks of the river. Montgomery had bought up some property no one else bid on ("when supposed to be on Government duty") and sold part of it next day for a healthy profit. People, said Waggoner, were beginning to imagine that the government was to blame when its officers behaved this way.

Three days later, Waggoner met Montgomery driving into the country while he himself was out on government business, and was outraged to discover later that the delinquent had been posting bills for private auctions when he should have been minding the Land Office during the temporary absence of the Government Agent, Mr McTaggart. "I am of the opinion," concluded Waggoner, more than a little pompously and, one suspects, with a soupçon of jealousy, "you will certainly agree . . . that such conduct of an official is lowering the character of the Civil Service. . . . It is unfair to all to allow an official to bring contempt and ridicule and walk around the streets making his boast that he has made independent of his salary since he left Battleford $1,550."

Within a week, Waggoner was dismayed to learn that Montgomery's "expected matrimonial alliance" was with Mr McTaggart's stepdaughter. There went any likelihood of McTaggart's support for his complaint. He was also dismayed to learn that the Commissioner proposed to allow Montgomery, in addition to his salary, a percentage on the collection of dues. Waggoner considered this to be a mistake: agents should be paid a straight salary. It was another nail in the coffin he would like to see prepared for Montgomery.

The Department of the Interior was probably heartily sick of its problem child Montgomery and probably also of gadfly Waggoner. However, another inquiry was ordered. Hugh was not dismissed. He continued with his job as forest ranger at Battleford, still on the books of the department in early 1890. At that time his request for four months' leave of absence was granted, "as this is the time of year at which Mr Montgomery's duties are lightest." He was planning to move his residence to

Prince Albert, his family now consisting of a wife and baby daughter Kate.

Leave of absence he may have had, but the papers are full of the strenuous rushing about he seems to have been doing, visiting as "an employee of the railway company," the tie camps and Duck Lake "to look after the interests of the Government among the tie contractors." In April the Prince Albert *Times* reported that "Mr Montgomery will return here with his wife and family, where he will reside in future."

The Prince Albert to which Maud was coming was a boom town. Officially designated a town five years earlier, in mid-1890 it boasted two bakeries, two hotels, two drugstores, two blacksmiths, two photographers, two jewellers, two breweries; a barber's shop, a millinery establishment, a sash and door factory, three butchers; one gunsmith, one tailor, one taxidermist; two gristmills (one waterpower, one steam-roller process) and three steam sawmills; one brickyard (another about to be established), two printing offices, three purveyors, four painters, five carpenter shops, seven bricklayers and masons; two doctors and a dentist, four law firms and one private bank. "Not a bad showing for a town situated as it has been, three hundred miles from a railway," said the *Times* complacently. The North-West Mounted Police division in the town, too, had recently organized a full brass band (it played at the Dominion Day celebrations attended by a thousand people— "no drunks and not a single arrest"), and sports were flourishing—lawn tennis, cricket, curling, baseball and lacrosse.

CHAPTER SIX

Prince Albert
year

On Friday, August 22, the *Times* announced that "Senator Montgomery of Prince Edward Island arrived here on Monday last. . . . He is accompanied by Miss Maude [*sic*] Montgomery, daughter of our esteemed townsman, H. J. Montgomery."

Three months earlier the travellers would have had to choose one of three routes into the town: by river steamer running between Winnipeg and Edmonton; by trail from Qu'Appelle Station (from which point the Royal Mail stage left every Wednesday); or by the Canadian Pacific Railway to Regina, changing there to the Regina and Prince Albert Railway as far as Saskatoon, "from which point conveyances may be had" for the remaining hundred miles. It was probably by the latter route that Maud reached the town. Nearly fifty years later she would comment that when she saw Saskatoon in 1890 it was "a railway station, a store and post-office and about half a dozen houses." In 1930, when she visited the West again, she found Saskatoon a university city.

The railway to Prince Albert was being pushed ahead so quickly that only three weeks after the arrival of the two Islanders the first through train arrived; and on the afternoon of October 24, Maud's unquenchable interest in significant events would surely have taken her into the crowd outside the newly plastered and painted station building, when the last spike of the Regina and Prince Albert Railway was driven by Lieutenant-Governor Royal.

Hugh Montgomery had added another occupation to his

busy schedule in August, when he was appointed one of several fisheries overseers (but without salary) with the powers of a Justice of the Peace. These additional duties may have kept him at home when his father continued his journey to the west coast, but he went with him nine days later as far as "the end of the track." Maud was left to get acquainted with her new family. The first heady excitement of a new environment would surely have needed a stronger word than the "int'resting" her little heroine Marigold would later use for the entrancing new experiences she was forever encountering. It never needed much to send Maud into raptures. "Oh, Susan, there is no such thing as a common day," her Anne would say in *Anne of Ingleside*. "Every day has something about it no other day has. Haven't you noticed?"

For Maud at this time there was the new young stepmother to size up, already three months pregnant with her second child. There was the little half-sister to love and cuddle—"the dearest sweetest prettiest little angel you can imagine," she wrote to her friend and cousin Penzie Macneill at the end of August. "She has a head covered with silky curls of the palest gold and big dark blue eyes so bright and sparkling." There was Prince Albert itself—had not her grandfather told the press he was "delighted with our town"?—not a flat prairie community, but set in a valley 1,400 feet above sea level, surrounded by forests and lakes and bluffs, and bisected by a satisfactory river where boats plied busily in summer and dog teams sped in winter. There was a new Presbyterian church, St Paul's, to attend, new friendships to make in high school. And there were *Indians*, romantic children of nature she could now see in the flesh—alas, not the brave, proud people she had expected, but a dispirited people walking the streets in poverty and distress.

But despite the novelties assaulting her senses from all sides, inevitable homesickness set in after Grandfather Montgomery had finally gone home after his return from the west coast— he was back in the Island at the end of September "looking hale and hearty," reported the Charlottetown *Patriot*. The recently discovered letters from teen-age Maud to her cousin Penzie complain of tedious baby-sitting chores, of the cranky

31

little half-brother Bruce, born in February 1891 ("the baby is so cross. Oh my! he is a terror. One of us has to have him in our arms the whole time"). There was disagreement, too, with her stepmother, who, only twenty-seven and a bit domineering, was finding some difficulty in coping with a highly sensitive girl on the edge of womanhood, and who seemed to regard her stepdaughter as a substitute for the servant she could not find. In fact, for nearly two months a resentful Maud was kept home to help with domestic chores, missing the education she was so anxious for (even though she wrote of "the dreadful place they call the high school" and wished it were "in Venezuela"). "I am ready to cut my throat in despair," she wrote in letters that ache with homesickness. "Oh I *couldn't* live another year in this place if I were paid a thousand dollars an hour."

Perhaps, too, Maud thought of her stepmother as a usurper. *Magic for Marigold,* written nearly forty years later, is shot through with a little girl's fear that her mother will allow some other man to take the place of her cherished dead father, though that mother was herself a second wife. Marigold, as possessive as Maud herself for her own, resented the replacement for the dead parent too.

It was a busy year for Hugh Montgomery. His multiplicity of jobs kept him on the run, rushing about the countryside ("Monty has very many warm friends here," said the Duck Lake correspondent), buying cattle and horses, land and railway ties, selling Confederation Life insurance policies since his appointment as local agent in the spring, arranging property sales, holding auctions of household goods, farm stock and implements. Toward the end of 1890 he was elected to the town council, and took his seat at the first meeting in January 1891. He was appointed to Finance Assessment, and became chairman of the Board of Works. He was also one of the managers of the Presbyterian church, and a dedicated member of the Saskatchewan Club curling team.

The weather was intermittently bad—"cold and rainy all the time, and the mud"—and "it is dreadful to be among strangers all the time," a heartfelt cry from a girl fresh from the warmth of close family ties. But Maud loved the tobogganning, and became almost swelled-headed from the reception her recitations received at local concerts. And if Maud was homesick, she had a refuge—"I was an indefatigable little scribbler"—and she could always escape into the ever fascinating world of writing, catching that elusive thought, or scene, or experience, in a net of words. In *Emily's Quest* she spoke for herself through her heroine: "A thing—an idea—whether of beauty or ugliness, tortured her until it was 'written out' . . . the comedy and tragedy of life enthralled her and demanded expression through her pen."

In this mood, and now recovered from the three-year setback after rejection, Maud wrote—in thirty-nine four-line verses—the legend of Cape Le Force, and sent it off to the *Patriot* in Charlottetown. Her grandfather Macneill had often told the story of the French sea-captain killed in a duel on the cape that now bore his name: legend of an earlier day, when Prince Edward Island was Ile-St-Jean and under the flag of France. Dividing up the gains ill-gotten from piracy on the high seas, while the ship lay anchored offshore and the men slept in tents on the headland, captain and mate quarrelled. In the duel fought next morning, the sneaky mate fired before the signal, while the ground was being paced off, and shot the captain dead. Assault by the waves on the soft sandstone of the cliffs had long since tumbled the grave into the ocean, but Grandfather could remember that *his* father had actually seen the spot where the captain lay buried.

The unbelievable happened. Father came home one night waving the *Patriot*—and there, on the front page of the issue of November 26, in a full column's worth of print, was Maud's epic, all thirty-nine verses, with her name in large capitals at the bottom. "It was the first sweet bubble on the cup of success and of course it intoxicated me." No matter that "some fearful printer's errors" made her cringe—misplaced apostrophes, omitted inverted commas, an *o* substituted for *e* that produced *repontance*, a *both* that should have been *loth*. No matter: it was *her* poem, and—at last!—in *print*. The idea of being paid for her work never entered the head of the young author. The prestige was enough.

More success was to follow. On June 17, 1891, the Prince

Albert *Times* published "A Western Eden, by Lucy Maud Montgomery," two and a third columns of her views on Saskatchewan in general and Prince Albert in particular.

As usual, what impressed Miss Montgomery were the scenic beauties of the little town "nestling at the foot of the terraced hills . . . and beyond it the vast sweep to the forest primeval . . . the level grassy meadows . . . picturesque bluffs which curve around, every few yards, to enclose a tiny blue lake . . . the magnificent river that rolls its blue tides freighted with the mysteries of former ages, past its poplar-fringed banks, with the busy little town on the one side and the unbroken forests of the northland on the other."

She spelt out her disappointment in the Indians. She had half-expected "to see a dusky warrior, clad in all his ancient panoply of war-paint and feathers, spring from [the] shadows, and ring his war-whoop over the waters of the river." But, alas, "the warrior never does appear . . . he belongs to an extinct species now." Nevertheless, Maud had great hopes for Saskatchewan—"a country where prosperity and freedom are awaiting thousands. . . . Hurrah for Saskatchewan!"

The sixteen-year-old author was further encouraged by seeing her article picked up by Winnipeg papers. The Manitoba *Evening Free Press and Sun* reprinted it as "the following excellent paper by Lucy Ward [sic] Montgomery . . . Words from the Pen of a Lady Writer." If the lady writer was not totally happy in Prince Albert, the year 1890-91 proved to be a lucky one for Maud's career. That winter saw publication of other articles and verses, including a prize-winning story in the Montreal *Witness*. She attended high school, made some lifelong friendships, and took her part as usual in church entertainments: before a packed audience in the Town Hall on January 30, Miss M. Montgomery gave a recitation at a special event by which the ladies of the Presbyterian church raised fifty-three dollars toward the new building planned for construction next summer.

It seems evident that Hugh Montgomery intended his eldest daughter to make her permanent home with him, now that he felt able to offer her one, but she was not comfortable in the renewed relationship and the call of the Island was too strong. He took her back to Cavendish in the summer of 1891. Yet gleams of happiness from that time persisted. More than twenty-five years later, when a friend glorying in "the yellow-ness and mellowness" of an October landscape in Saskatche-wan regretted that she had not seen and described it, she replied: "I never left any description of it, I believe, but I saw it—oh, I saw it . . . that year in Prince Albert that I spent with father. Never shall I forget it. I used to soak my soul in it. I believe people call me a cheery person who 'brings a gift of laughter'. If so I think it should be attri-buted to that self-same western golden-ness which penetrated my being so deeply in that far-off magic month that even amid to-day's middle-aged grayness some stray gleams and embers are visible."

And the grandeur of Saskatchewan storms, though they terrified her at the time, stayed in her memory. "I remember how frightened I was by my first Western thunderstorm when I was a girl of fifteen used only to the much milder storms of the Maritimes. I positively *crouched*. It seemed as if every simultaneous crash and flash must rend the house in pieces."

She gave at least one story a Prince Albert setting—*Tannis of the Flats*, published in *Further Chronicles of Avonlea* in 1920—though it lacks any vivid background of the area.

In early 1891, while Maud was on her western visit, her father ran for the federal parliament as a Liberal. The Prince Albert *Times*, strongly Conservative, supported his opponent, D. H. Macdowall. "People are astonished at an old Conserva-tive like Montgomery turning Grit so suddenly, and want ex-planations which will have to be very clear before proving satisfactory." Both candidates published addresses to the elec-tors based on a platform in which many of the planks were the same. The point of divergence was the issue of "unre-stricted reciprocity between Canada and the United States and the free interchange of products, both natural and manu-factured." It was a policy that would divide Canadian think-ing for years to come.

The *Times* reported "enthusiastic meetings" and "rousing receptions" for the Conservative candidate. But as for "poor

Monty," there was commiseration. "His reception was decidedly frigid. . . . Four years ago he fed at the Government expense and now they refuse to employ him." (Did Waggoner finally get rid of his bugbear after that second inquiry?) "Let us warn Monty and his ultra grit friends that he cannot consistently stroke the American eagle with one hand and with the other pull the British Lion's tail. We pity Monty, he has been made a tool of."

Nevertheless, "Monty" was a popular local figure, and even the *Times* sugared the pill with some compliments. He was "a man of boyant [*sic*] spirits, full of hope and a belief in man's honesty, [who] was induced by stuffed telegrams to enter the contest. . . . Mr Montgomery made a strong figure, and, unlike many of his supporters, will take his defeat like a man."

In the eight years that followed before his death, Maud's association with her father can have been little more than an exchange of letters, though perhaps he occasionally came east to visit his native province. For all his energy and enterprise, Hugh Montgomery does not seem to have been highly successful in any of his jack-of-all-trades undertakings. Although in her mid-fifties Maud would stand by his grave in Prince Albert and remember "I loved my father very very deeply. He was the most lovable man I ever met," the ties between them had stretched very thin. The host of fatherless children who rise from her pages treasuring their memories of a lost and idealized parent may reflect a subconscious resentment that her father had been lost to her by his own act: had, in effect, deserted her and denied her the security she clearly wanted and needed by removing himself from her life and handing her into the care of grandparents far removed from her in age and temperament. Security, in fact, she did not lack: but the need of this warm and responsive child to feel close, to be wanted, was rebuffed by her father's departure and may well have been responsible for the wall of reserve she would soon begin to build around her emotions.

Hugh John Montgomery died of pneumonia at Prince Albert on January 16, 1900, at the age of fifty-eight. In the years since his eldest daughter had returned to Prince Edward Island, Hugh Montgomery had continued to play his forceful part in community life. As town councillor he had been defeated after one year in office, but he had continued to find "ample scope," as the Prince Albert *Times* put it, for "his indomitable business enterprise," filling "many positions of trust, municipal and financial, with his characteristic ability and efficiency." Among these was the post of town jailer.

His obituary regretted the loss of "a man of extraordinary energy, enterprising ability and of sterling uprightness and strength of character." Another half-brother and -sister for Maud, Carlyle and Ila, had been added to Kate and Bruce, the two babies she had known. Their mother would die in 1910 at the age of forty-seven.

CHAPTER SEVEN

Schoolteacher

Maud spent the winter of her return to the Island at Park Corner, giving music lessons and writing poems, and more poems, for the *Patriot*. Perhaps it was now, beset by the passionate urgings of adolescence and better able to understand romantic love, that she may have re-read Lytton's *Zanoni*, weaving her daydreams around that intense and masterful figure.

"Zanoni!" she wrote in 1936, half-amused by her youthful passion, half-haunted still by that magic memory. Such a lush, flamboyant allegory, in which the good are noble beyond belief, the bad bestial beyond saving, was well calculated to attract a mind already half in love with mysticism and reaching for a beauty that *must* exist beyond earthly understanding, beyond the fragile veil. Its esoteric Rosicrucian philosophy hinted at secrets of unimaginable splendour attainable only by the pure and the steadfast. The high-sounding, second-person-singular dialogue carried overtones of poetic grandeur, removing its human participants far from any link with reality. Maud, already a seasoned traveller in fairyland, found this new realm only one stage beyond familiar territory.

The writing was authentic Maud-language. "Since his dark eyes have haunted me," cries Viola after meeting the mysterious Zanoni, "I am no longer the same. I long to escape from myself—to glide with the sunbeam over the hill tops—to become something that is not of earth. . . ."

"Thou only, methinks, in all the earth [Zanoni to Viola]

hast the power to wound or delight me!" Rapturous Viola: "Mould me to what thou wilt...."

Attainment of the final power meant standing fast against the dread Haunter of the Threshold: after which, magical powers and "a sense of unearthly delight—of an existence that seemed all spirit"—would reward the transformed soul. Maud recalled being so wildly in love with Zanoni "that local beaus had no chance"—probably, she said, saving her from a lot of silly "calf" affairs. She learned whole chapters of the book by heart, and rewrote some of it herself to make the heroine rise to Zanoni's stature. "I thought her silly, weak and unworthy of him ... I could never forgive her for her desertion of him." Maud would never have deserted him. She wrote herself in as Viola, "but not the Viola of the book.... In my version we were parted, but not through any fault of our own, and at last we escaped the Terror [of the French Revolution] and fled back to our own isle."

At times she was not Viola, nor in love with Zanoni, but a pupil of Mejnour the Master Mystic, one of the immortals. Unlike the Englishman Glyndon, who had succumbed to the delights of temptation, and failed the final test, Maud would be a pupil who passed the Threshold and "attained the great secret—the first woman who ever 'passed the Order.'" Sometimes she added a "codicil," making Mejnour appear suddenly in the last chapter, adopt Zanoni's child, and bring it up to be a second Zanoni. "It always worried me terribly to think of that poor baby alone in the world, especially the world of the Terror."

With this kind of romantic dreaming, despite the stinging disappointment of rejection by the New York *Sun* of a story she had sent some months earlier, she "scribbled" during her year at Park Corner and then returned to school at Cavendish to prepare for the entrance examination to Prince of Wales College in Charlottetown. At the college during a winter of study for a teacher's certificate (she received a Second Class Certificate in 1894), she received the first payment for any of her writing—two subscriptions to an American magazine for her poem *Only A Violet*. Around 1927, she gave a group of

Presbyterian ministers and their wives in Hamilton, Ontario, another version of her first payment—the choice of seeds to the value of fifty cents. This was the version she used for Emily of New Moon's first success. Whichever payment came first for Maud herself, "It is a start," she recorded jubilantly in her journal, "and I mean to keep on. Oh, I wonder if I shall ever be able to do anything worth while in the way of writing. It is my dearest ambition."

But more than yearning is needed to achieve ambition. "When people say to me, as they occasionally do, 'Oh, how I envy you your gift, how I wish I could write as you do,' I am inclined to wonder, with some inward amusement, how much they would have envied me on those dark, cold, winter mornings of my apprenticeship." For dark and cold they were when she was boarding at a Bideford farmhouse during the year of teaching that followed.

Maud Montgomery, uncertain of her talent but determined not to lodge it useless, had courage and tenacity. Finding her creative genius dulled after weary hours of teaching, she would rise at six o'clock, dressing by lamplight. Wrapped in a heavy coat, with feet tucked under her to keep them warm, she would write for an hour with frozen fingers in a frozen house where yesterday's ashes still lay in the grate.

After her year of teaching at Bideford on the Island, she decided to enter Dalhousie College (now Dalhousie University) for a special course in literature under Professor Archibald MacMechan, and spent the following winter in Halifax, Nova Scotia. The course was a delight to her, but perhaps the real highlight of that period was the "Big Week" that occurred during her stay. Monday of Big Week saw the arrival of a cheque for five dollars from *Golden Days* of Philadelphia, for a juvenile story (the magazine failed later, and "I don't know whether my stories killed it or not," she quipped). On Wednesday, she was awarded the Halifax *Evening Mail*'s five-dollar prize for the best letter on "Which has the greater patience—man or woman?" On Saturday, twelve dollars arrived for a poem sent to *Youth's Companion*. No wonder she became known in the college as "the girl who writes stories and poems for the magazines and gets paid for them."

Her prize "letter" had been submitted in the form of verses written at three o'clock in the morning (a room-mate remembers her nocturnal risings to jot down ideas and lines of poems). She took her first five dollars and spent it on lasting remembrances of her triumph: five volumes of poetry—Tennyson, Byron, Milton, Longfellow and Whittier.

She may have been responsible also for two articles appearing in the *Dalhousie Gazette*. The first, *The Bad Boy of Blanktown*, published in the issue of 4 March 1896, and signed L.M.M., is almost certainly her work, an amusing anecdote by someone who has been a teacher, and marked by her happy knack of pungent phrasing. . . . *As for his mouth— you could have cut mouths for a dozen boys from it and still have a good piece left over . . . George's voice . . . was of great compass, was cracked in three distinct places, and regularly fell all to pieces at the end of every sentence, when he was reading.* The second piece, a letter to *Dear Gazette* in the March 20 issue and signed *Maud*, is less recognizably hers, though light-hearted and whimsical.

She received her First Class Licence for teaching on July 23, 1895, four months before her twenty-first birthday. During two more years of teaching, first at Belmont Lot 16 and then at Lower Bedeque, she "grubbed away industriously . . . and ground out stories and verses on days so hot that I feared my very marrow would melt and my gray matter be hopelessly sizzled up. But oh, I love my work! I love spinning stories, and I love to sit by the window of my room and shape some 'airy fairy' fancy into verse."

Many of them were published, and she added more markets to her list of those she had "sold." Her only regret was the necessity of dragging a moral into juvenile stories. "The kind of juvenile story I like best to write—and read, too, for the matter of that—is a good, jolly one, 'art for art's sake', or rather 'fun for fun's sake', with no insidious moral hidden away in it like a pill in a spoonful of jam!"

In March 1898 Grandfather Macneill died at the age of almost seventy-eight. Maud gave up teaching and returned to Cavendish, where her grandmother was now alone. Her Uncle John, who lived on the next lot, ran his own and now also his father's farm; the womenfolk attended to the household chores. When Lucy Macneill was appointed postmistress in her dead husband's place, Maud became her assistant.

Maud remained at Cavendish for the next thirteen years until her grandmother's death in March 1911, except for nearly a year, from the fall of 1901 until June 1902, when she went to Halifax and became "the *Echo* proof-reader and general handy-man!"—the *Daily Echo* being an evening edition of the Halifax *Chronicle*.

"I'm a newspaper woman!" she wrote in her journal.

CHAPTER EIGHT

Newspaperwoman

The *Echo* could hardly have chosen better for its newspaper-woman. She was quick, she was versatile, she was used to labouring over words and phrases, she was cheerful, and—as Ephraim Weber, the correspondent whose lifelong friendship with Maud would begin this very year, commented after her death—she would never produce "a single careless or perfunctory line."

In the rush of newspaper production, errors could creep in, however much care was taken, "and then there is mischief to pay . . . headlines wildly askew and editorials hopelessly hocussed": but few could have done better at the job than Maud, with her care for detail. Proofreading, "although tedious," she actually enjoyed. In Saturday editions she became editor of the society page, sometimes required to fake a social report when an out-of-town correspondent's letter failed to materialize. This she disliked, but she had no real trouble in producing when necessary. She wrote ironically: "Poor Miss Montgomery goes meekly to work, and concocts an introductory paragraph or so about 'autumn leaves' and 'mellow days' and 'October frosts', or any old stuff like that to suit the season. Then I go carefully over the columns of the weekly, clip out all the available personals and news items, about weddings, and engagements, and teas, etc., hash them up in epistolary style, forge the Windsor correspondent's nom de plume —and there's your society letter! I used to include funerals, too, but I found the news editor blue-pencilled them. Evidently funerals have no place in society."

On Mondays she was Cynthia, who wrote *Around the Tea*

Table, "a column or so of giddy paragraphs." At Christmas, she was required to visit firms that advertised in the *Echo,* and boil down for a free write-up the impressions gained from interview and inspection. This was another job she disliked, but at least on one occasion it paid off. Promised a new hat if the Bon Marché millinery establishment was well boosted, she was agreeably surprised to find that the promise was not a joke. "Sure enough . . . up came the hat, and a very pretty one it is too."

Not for nothing did Maud call herself the *Echo*'s general handyman. "All the odd jobs that go a-begging in this office are handed to the present scribe." When the ending of a story was lost after half the copy had been set, she was pressed into completing it. In real life she never heard whether the original author saw the superimposed ending. In *Emily's Quest,* she made good use of the incident, creating an eccentric writer who came breathing the fire of outraged authorship and stayed to propose marriage. But she did encounter one aftermath of an assignment to tighten up a draggy serial, "cutting out most of the kisses and embraces, two-thirds of the love-making, and all the descriptions": a month later, a conversation overheard on a streetcar almost convulsed her.

"Two ladies beside me were discussing the serial that had just ended in the *Echo.* 'You know,' said one, 'it was the strangest story I ever read. It wandered on, chapter after chapter, for weeks, and never seemed to get anywhere; and then it just finished up in eight chapters, lickety-split. I can't understand it!' "

Although the paper went to press at two-thirty, routine duties kept Maud in the office until six o'clock to answer phones, accept telegrams, cope with extra proofs; often sitting alone, but with noise all around. "Overhead, in the composing room, they are rolling machines and making a diabolical noise. . . . In the inner office two reporters are having a wrangle."

It was a busy, tiring, grubby year. "This office is really the worst place for getting dirty I ever was in." She found herself too tired at night to do more than darn stockings and sew on buttons. Early rising was no solution: the hours she had to

*Cavendish Capes on the northern curve of the Island was half
a mile from the Macneill homestead. "... a silver surf ...
dashing on the sands in a splendid white turmoil," wrote
Maud. "Oh, the glory of that far gaze across the tossing
waters."*

The house at Clifton (now New London) where Maud was born is now an L.M. Montgomery museum.

Clifton (New London), where L.M. Montgomery was born on 30 November 1874

Courtesy Mrs Ruth Campbell

Public Archives of Canada

Hugh John Montgomery, Maud's father, with his second wife, Mary Ann McRae

Senator Donald Montgomery, Maud's paternal grandfather

Courtesy Mrs Ruth Campbell

Courtesy Mrs Ruth Campbell

Grandfather Alexander Macneill

Grandmother Lucy Woolner Macneill

*Four generations:
Grandmother Macneill; her
son the Reverend Leander
Macneill; his son Professor
Murray Macneill (brother
of Ken) and his daughter
Edith*

*Rear view of the old
Macneill homestead (no
longer standing) which lay
between two orchards full
of apple and cherry trees.
The post office entrance
was at the front.*

"ARK CORNER", RES. OF HON. DON. MONTGOMERY, PARK CORNER, LOT 21 P. E. I.

At eleven, Maud was already an inveterate scribbler, an imaginative child with "a passport to fairyland."

At sixteen, Maud spent a year with her father in Prince Albert.

At nineteen, Maud was studying for her Second Class teachers' certificate at Prince of Wales College.

*Maud Montgomery
in the mid-1890s,
aged about
twenty-five*

Maud, aged twenty-eight. Two years later, in 1904, she earned $591.85 from her writing.

work made the early-to-bed of her schoolma'am days impossible. If she were to write at all, she would have to squeeze odd minutes from a day beset with the noise of machines and loud voices and telephone bells, interrupted by galleys to be proofread, people to be interviewed, writing assignments to be completed. "All my spare time here I write, and not such bad stuff either, since the *Delineator*, the *Smart Set* and *Ainslies'* have taken some of it. I have grown accustomed to stopping in the middle of a paragraph to interview a prowling caller, and to pausing in full career after an elusive rhyme, to read a lot of proof, and snarled-up copy."

She was now about to discover that her precious words were not being loosed on the unresponsive air. Poems published in the national magazines of North America were read and cherished by a network of ardent souls who sought, and often found, a response to their own yearning for beauty in thought and word: many of them, like Maud herself, making their own lonely and often defeated attempts to trap ideas and experiences in elusive rhyme. Among such as these, the need to communicate with others they thought they recognized as kindred spirits often expressed itself in spontaneous letters of appreciation and respect.

Living in Philadelphia and numbered among these literary dabblers, a lady named Miriam Zieber had become an indefatigable collector of pen friends, Maud among them. She belonged to (and may have initiated) a writers' club established for just this purpose—to put in touch by letter people who shared similar cultural interests. In March 1902, a letter came to Cavendish from Ephraim Weber, a bachelor homesteader in Alberta, who for some time past had been attracted by poems from the pen of a person he supposed was *Mr* L. M. Montgomery. His impression corrected by Miss Zieber, he was urged to write to *Miss* Montgomery, who belonged to Cavendish, Prince Edward Island, but who was for the moment living and working in Halifax.

Weber's first letter was bald and brief, without salutation other than name and address at the head of the page. "Miss Zieber says I am to write to you. She tells me she has obtained permission for me to do so, and that she is sure a correspondence between us would give us both much pleasure and literary edification. The idea is altogether hers, and I hope she is right." He told Maud he liked those of her poems he had seen; hoped to see more; had himself had a few small things printed; looked forward to hearing from her.

Weber, thirty-one when the correspondence started, was brought up in Waterloo County, Ontario, Canadian-born into a Pennsylvania German Mennonite farm background. He was twelve years old before he spoke any English. There had been little culture in either his heredity or the farm environment of his youth; he deeply envied Maud her childhood of books and reading. At nineteen he had gone back to school with children little more than half his age and continued through high school to Normal School. Then, after discovering that teaching was an uncongenial occupation, he decided to follow his family to western Canada. His grandfather had founded the town of Didsbury, Alberta, in the early 1890s. Weber took up a homestead tract nearby and found the work healthy and satisfying, except—in his hunger for music and culture—for its isolation. His literary pen-friendships and his literary scribblings were a reaching-out to the wider world of the intellect.

In the first few years, at least until *Anne of Green Gables* soared to totally unexpected heights of fame and Maud's time fell victim to the demands of publisher and public, as many as half a dozen letters a year were exchanged between Maud and Weber. As responsibilities made heavier demands on them both, the exchanges dwindled in frequency, though not in length. Maud's letters turned into journal-like packages running up to thirty-odd pages in her sprawling handwriting, started in a free moment, put aside for days—sometimes weeks —and continued when time permitted.

She had her twenty-seventh birthday in Halifax, and spent a Christmas not as lonely as she had feared, dining at the Halifax Hotel with a friend and attending a performance of Barrie's *Little Minister*. March 30 found her writing up the Easter Sunday parade after a week of fog and rain and neuralgia. She was now selling quite regularly to such markets as the *Sunday School Times*, the *Family Herald, Current Litera-ture, Youth's Companion*. But poetry was always her first love. In her spare time, she continued doggedly to grind out what she called pot-boilers—"various blameless rhymes for a con-sideration of filthy lucre," but many of them still earned only the prestige of publication. She yearned with a painful and unfulfilled longing for the touch of genius capable of produc-ing the grand power and sweep of words that went to her heart from the pages of Byron, Tennyson, Arnold—knowing full well that this further gift would be forever denied her. Of Emerson's "poet," the *fated man of men whom the ages must obey*, she wrote regretfully, "*I* shall never hear that random word. My ear is not attuned to its lofty thunder."

"Her own efforts were naive," writes her son. But she tried. "I've written one real poem out of my heart," she recorded in a week when pot-boilers were in the majority. But even the poem out of her heart never achieved greatness.

She plodded on with stories, both juvenile and adult, sell-ing chiefly to United States publications because they paid best, but occasionally breaking into the journals of her own country. One of her earliest stories, *Kismet*, was published in *The Canadian Magazine* of July 1899. Slight and sentimental, in which (as a modern critic has commented) she proved her-self to be "mistress of the cliché," it was nevertheless a vig-nette not wholly unworthy, written during her apprentice-ship and showing a glimmering of her peculiar ability to take the reader beyond the moment and behind the mask: the ability to picture the before and after of the particular mo-ment on which she was casting her spotlight; to make her reader see more aspects of her characters than those she sets out in the words on her pages. But it is a contrived story—the chance meeting of an estranged husband and wife at a horse race on whose outcome they impulsively place the decision to take up life together again—written for a commercial market by one who, as she freely admitted, expected only to "attain to a recognized position among the everyday workers of my time." She had not yet found her true talent as the authentic recorder of childhood aspirations and anxieties. Much of her writing, especially at this time, was sentimental, romantic, fey, often painfully contrived, sometimes downright silly, with forced humour and farcical situations. In 1906 she commented on a serial being written to order, "It is a very sensational yarn, written to suit the taste of the journal that ordered it and I don't care much for writing such but they offer a good price for it. It deals with a lost ruby, a lunatic, an idiot boy, a mysterious turret chamber and a lot of old standard truck like that." Even when she had matured, her short stories were never very successful, and her books retain much of her sentimentality, but she was honest enough to recognize her limitations, even though—like all true writers—she hoped one day to produce something memorable, even great. Although she never achieved greatness, some of her books became memorable.

"She was the first to admit that her writings were not great literature," writes her son Stuart, "and also that they did not spring to life through any inspiration, but were the result of constant observation, note-taking, phrase-making and hard work. However, I know that her main source of strength was the knowledge that she came up the hard way by her own efforts, with never in her life violating her personal and professional integrity in the most minute way."

CHAPTER NINE

Pen-friendships

In June 1902, Maud returned to Cavendish, to join her grandmother again. Her life during the next eight years, apart from
the writing that to her was certainly its most important occupation, was the daily round of necessary chores—housecleaning, painting, sewing ("non-excitably nice"), cooking (which
she liked), gardening (which she loved)—that were the lot of
almost all countrywomen of the day: in her case, illumined by
her private visions and special responses to every scene and
every event. Homecoming to orchards in full bloom was like
"an exquisite drink" to Maud. "Have you become sober yet
from the lily fragrance?" asked Weber.

In her early letters—and indeed threaded through her later
ones—are bursts of rare delight in the beauties of nature, in
the kernel of laughter at the heart of a trivial incident, in that
flash of the spirit—Emily's flash—that so often uplifted her. "It
was like being born again to see the drifts go and the catkins
bud on the willows. I know exactly what I shall feel like on
the resurrection morning! . . . The woods are getting ready
to sleep—they are not yet asleep but they are disrobing and
are having all sorts of little bed-time conferences and whisper-
ings and good-nights. . . .

" . . . Thermometer 5 below zero. A raging snowstorm to
boot. Frost on window panes. Wind wailing in chimney. A
box of white Roman hyacinths sending out alien whiffs of old
summers.

" . . . Three evenings ago I went to the shore. We had a wild
storm of wind and rain the day before but this evening was
clear, cold, with an air of marvellous purity. The sunset was

lovely beyond words . . . my soul was filled with a nameless exhilaration. . . . The woods are human but the sea is of the company of the archangels. . . ."

The letters were full, too, of the curiosity of a questing mind. *What is your conception of an angel? Are you the owner of a Spanish castle? What do you think of the spelling reform agitation? Have you read* Through Science by Faith *by Norman Smith? . . . Jack London's* Sea Wolf? . . . *Gibbon's* Decline and Fall? . . . The Law of Psychic Phenomena? . . . *Yes, I have read Trench's* Study of Words . . . *Congratulations on discovering—the Bible!*

In mid-1903, Maud was once again the beneficiary of Miriam Zieber's literary ambitions. Another of Miriam's correspondents was a young man who lived in Alloa in the county of Clackmannan, Scotland. George Boyd MacMillan, then aged twenty-two, was an apprentice printer with the *Alloa Advertiser*; a year later, having taught himself shorthand, he joined the *Alloa Journal* as a reporter, where he had a long and respected career. He, too, was an aspiring writer, and at the age of seventeen he had won first prize for Scotland in a national essay competion on "Our Queen," followed by a moderate success in various British journals.

Miss Zieber had by now conceived an optimistic plan: a community of writers, set up for mutual aid. She had already persuaded Weber to move to Philadelphia. "I keep house for myself and board a friend, Mr Weber," she had written to MacMillan on July 10. " . . . Lately I am [having] one tiny success after another, and so is Mr Weber. We are, therefore, much encouraged." She then launched into her pet project, with dubious spelling and grammar. "*Say*, cannot you come over here? . . . There is a darling wish very close to my heart for many a day: that of forming an exclusive circle of writers for entirely unselfish helpfulness towards each member. So far I am sure of the quality of character for this purpose of only you, Mr Weber, a young lady of superior ability living on Prince Edward's Island, and myself. My plan is to take in no one who is not willing to freely give his or her very best help to all the other members. We three have already aided one another finely, for some time past, but we are not organized. There would be no money in the case, only a full understanding and Christian love and kindness. It will be better to keep the circle small. I'll broach the matter to Miss Montgomery, and if she consents I'll give you an introduction to her and you'll find her a most delightful correspondent. She is ahead of us, is working her way, slowly, into some of our best magazines. She is best on verse. Writes sketches and stories too. . . . I wish to restrict the circle to ten or a dozen members, and I will want to claim the right to accept, or reject candidates for admission, as I have studdied human character deeply and feel fully able to choose discreetly. . . . What do you think of the plan?"

Apparently no one thought much of it. Eventually even Weber gave up and returned to Canada. But some time between July and November of 1903, MacMillan wrote to Maud, who replied on December 29 to say she would be "very pleased to carry on a literary correspondence with you and hope we can make it mutually helpful and interesting." For reasons that puzzled her, Miss Zieber had asked her not to mention MacMillan to Weber, and she faithfully did not. But "she did not put any prohibition on my mentioning him to you." Weber, she explained, was also a writer, and "very clever . . . you missed a good thing in not capturing [him] as a correspondent. He is A-1 in that respect and writes most delightful epistles."

MacMillan, too, wrote most delightful epistles to this pen-friend whose name had come to him through the happy chance of Miss Zieber's eccentricities. "I remember well," another Alloa man, Roy Carmichael, wrote to MacMillan in 1951, "when we joined that American writers' club which furnished you with L.M.M. as a correspondent, and me with a Kansas City man of whom after a few years I lost track, and whose name I do not even remember. You were fortunate in that long literary and friendly acquaintance."

Perhaps the vagaries of Carmichael's memory caused him to confuse Weber with the Kansas City man. At any rate, Maud was vastly intrigued to discover in 1905 that Weber had a Scottish journalist on his list. He turned out to be Carmichael, who later became an active press correspondent in Montreal until his death in 1954.

The friendship with both Weber and MacMillan lasted for

forty years, until Maud's death brought it to an end. Miss Zieber, the catalyst, faded away into obscurity within a few years, marrying a Mr Watrous—"an architect or contractor or something of the sort." Though they were always formally addressed as "My dear Mr Weber/MacMillan," though Maud and Weber married other partners, though she met Weber briefly in the flesh only three times, MacMillan only once (but that once a span of a couple of weeks), these two men may have given her the most intense and happy relationships of her life. "What a wonderful thing our friendship has been," she would tell MacMillan thirty years later. " . . . It seems to me something predestined . . . I realize how much would have been lacking in my life had this correspondence never materialized."

Though other needs and other values were satisfied by other relationships, Maud Montgomery's questioning mind and strong literary interests found in her correspondence with both men a richly rewarding experience. To MacMillan she opened out even more than to Weber; they were both "kindred spirits," but MacMillan was nearer to her own spiritual wavelength.

"I am 26 years old," she told him in this first letter (she was actually twenty-nine—did she feel that a young man of twenty-two might be intimidated by her seven-year seniority?), "and like yourself have been scribbling all my life. Six years ago I began to inflict my scribblings on a public that suffereth long and is kind. I have got on well and make a comfortable living for one small girl by my pen, besides finding a vast deal of pleasure in my work."

Miss Zieber thought her prose was poor. "But I am frankly in literature to make my living out of it. My prose sells and so I write it, although I prefer writing verse. I know that I can never be a really great writer. My aspiration is limited to this —I want to be a *good workman* in my chosen profession. I cannot be one of the masters but I hope to attain to a recognized position among the everyday workers of my time." She had made five hundred dollars this year, one hundred only of which had been for verse.

Though it might be thought a bit egotistical, she felt it

necessary—"especially at the start"—to describe herself for her new correspondent. "Apart from my literary bent I am small, said to be very vivacious, and am very fond of fun and good times generally . . . I am interested in many things and *love living*. I have a camera and enjoy taking photos [she did her own processing] . . . I love *fancy-work*, CATS, horses, pretty dresses and feminine things generally. Revel in books. Don't go in for athletics but love out-of-doors."

In these early letters, Maud gave MacMillan useful information about markets in North America: what editors wanted, length of articles, payment. She sent him copies of her poems. He returned envelopes "fat with clippings and postcards" and some of his *Journal* pieces: Maud liked his "interview" with a sea serpent. He too loved the outdoors. Over the years he sent long and deeply appreciated accounts of holidays spent in various scenic areas of Britain.

They plunged straight into the same animated discussions Maud had been enjoying with Weber: about literature, the possibility of life after death, reincarnation, fairies. *Is discontent helpful to development? Do old people take life less seriously than the young? Why does a trivial event often influence a life more strongly than an important one? Surely all beauty contains a spark of the divine? Is sin in the motive or the act? Will we ever be able to carry out our good resolutions?* ("The next day after never, dear friend," said wise Maud.)

"There is something I want to say right here," she wrote. "If our correspondence is to be really a help and inspiration to each other it is necessary above all else that it should be perfectly frank and sincere. We must feel that we are perfectly free to write as we will, without fear of shocking the other by heresy in any views, spiritual or temporal. You may ask me any question you wish on any subject and I will answer as freely and frankly as there may be light in me to do. Only thus, I think, can a correspondence between people personally unknown be mutually helpful and interesting. In personal intercourse conventional disguises may serve a good and kindly purpose in promoting harmony but I hold them unnecessary in such a friendship as ours."

They exchanged postcards of favourite views (Maud preserved his as bookmarks), copies of favourite poems, clippings of amusing or provocative anecdotes that immediately sparked repartee. Maud sent him a maple leaf, a box of red rose leaves; he sent her a sprig of heather, some flowers which she wore in her hair to a concert, a bit of tansy from the grave of the Black Dwarf. "I could not have been more delighted if you had sent me a whole Scottish 'loch,' " she exclaimed, enchanted. With typical whimsy she went out and bought a copy of Sir Walter Scott's novel "to be able to paste the tansy on the title page!" as she commented to Weber when rejoicing in this gift from "a friend in Scotland," faithfully not naming him.

As the years passed and letters between them became less frequent, but longer, she would write with her diary before her, catching up on events since her last letter, posing some literary or philosophical query, seeking comment on some elusive thought or emotion. Many passages in letters to both men read almost word for word, but to MacMillan she wrote in greater detail and with more intimate revelations of her life's joys and sorrows.

CHAPTER TEN

Behind
the mask

These were not easy years for Maud, though her letters speak of occasional holidays of a month at a time away from home. Nothing in real life ever came up to her early dreams except the world of nature. Maud took possession of earth's beauties and made them her own. Beauty ravished her soul, and wherever else life might fail her, this stood firm to the end.

"When I grew up out of that strange dreamy childhood of mine and went out into the world of reality, I met with experiences that bruised my spirit," she wrote to MacMillan. " . . . The outward circumstances of my life are at present miserably circumscribed and carking—owing in great measure to poor old Grandmama's set ways of age and rapidly increasing childishness. . . ." But she had her retreat. "I am sometimes lonely in the house or when walking with uncongenial company, but I have never known a moment's loneliness in the woods and fields. I have ripe, rich, rare good company there. . . ."

She was fast learning the ability to disguise her real feelings that would stand her in good stead in the years to come—to wear a public face that said nothing of what she felt and thought. "As a rule, I am very careful to be shallow and conventional where depth and originality are wasted. When I get very desperate I retreat into realms of cloudland. . . . I learned that that world and the real world clashed hopelessly and irreconcilably, and I learned to keep them apart so that the former might remain for me unspoiled. I learned to meet other people on their own ground since there seemed to be no meeting place on mine. I learned to hide my thoughts and dreams and fancies that had no place in the strife and clash of the market place. I found that it was useless to look for kindred souls in the multitude. . . ."

At the same time, she was casting an introspective eye on her own personality, and though she might rebel against much of Grandma's Calvinism, some of it stuck. "The trials of an uncongenial environment should be regarded as discipline," she wrote earnestly in March 1906. "I have been led to this conclusion by the marked influence my external surroundings and the life I have had to live for the past eight years has had upon my character. I see now plainly that I *needed* the training very much and that it has done me much good in many ways but chiefly in enabling me to form habits of self-control. I used to be a most impulsive, passionate creature. I do not use the word passionate in the sense of temper," she amended hastily, "for that is not one of my besetting sins. But I used always to *rush to extremes* in any emotion, whether of hatred, affection, ambition, or what not, that came uppermost. It was a very serious defect and injurious to me in many ways, mentally, morally, physically. . . . I cannot certainly say that it has been eradicated. I fear that, given favorable circumstances, it might blaze up as strongly as ever. But it certainly has been much modified and as a consequence I am a much more comfortable person to others and to myself. . . ."

In her self-examination Maud found an entirely understanding friend in MacMillan, who was struggling with the idea that his gift for humour was at war with his religious ideals—its use possibly too flippant for the real and earnest business of living. Maud had cheerful words for him. "I *do* think that we are *always* justified . . . in doing what comes easiest and best for us to do. Do not fear that it is selfish to embark in a life that 'brings the greatest good to yourself alone'. . . . Any life that brings good to yourself must bring good first to other people—and that is enough, even if it be only the good of a laugh, a smile, a moment's relief from the cark and care of existence. . . . You have possibly too narrow a view of what religion really is—perhaps you are too much inclined to regard the *letter* as religion instead of the spirit.

I do not think that you need feel worry because the line of work you take up may not be the highest."

An earlier comment proved to be apt. "I think I would have made a good *preacher*. Only, when I got up in the pulpit, and saw facing me rows upon rows of dull, unresponsive faces, unlit by a single flame . . . of feeling, all my fine sentiments would probably collapse like a punctured balloon and I would come down flat."

To Weber in 1905 she wrote: "There are two distinct sides to my nature. When I go to the woods the dreamy, solitary side comes uppermost and I love the woods best. But when I mingle with other people quite another aspect rules me. I am very fond of society, sparkling conversation, the good *human* times of life. . . . But as to being only 'two of me' as you ask . . . there's a hundred of me . . . some of the 'me's' are good, some *not*. It's better than being just two or three, I think—more exciting, more interesting."

One of the *me's* was the Maud Montgomery few people saw. Witty, vivid and *alive* her letters showed her to be. But she also wrote to Weber of sick headaches, nervous spells; and of unorthodox religious views that must have been simmering behind her controlled public face. She was not—or at any rate was no longer—the bubbly Anne-child of her books. The rapturous, magic childhood had been diminished by reality, though it remained alive in the secret places of her heart and would burst out joyfully in the books by which she would be remembered.

She drew in on herself all the more because she was steadily growing disillusioned by human nature. "People waste any amount of gray matter and nervous energy toeing the chalk-lines prescribed by conventionalities and Mrs Grundy." (Nevertheless, she would toe them herself pretty strictly in days to come, despite her silent inner protest.) "I think the majority of people are prosaic and unideal. . . . The other evening, sitting by myself at the window of my den in the twilight . . . I amused myself by counting up the number of people I knew whom I thought to be really happy. The number was fearfully small—so small that it quite reconciled me to being myself, although a few moments before that I had been full of rebellious discontent, questioning of whys and wherefores."

People who knew her then, those who knew her later in other circumstances and environments, remember her as an outgoing personality, ready with conversation and laughter. She had told MacMillan that she was said to be vivacious, but she also told him that she was not "brilliant and epigrammatic" in conversation. "In *general* company I'm really a dull mortal—having nothing to say and saying it flatly. It is only in a circle where I feel thoroughly at home that I can sparkle at all." When she had become a public figure, she won a reputation for wit and gaiety. She had become more adept by then at sparkling, even when there was no real fire: even when the sparkle covered an aching heart and a weary spirit and tired body.

She took an active part in the Cavendish Literary Society, as secretary, as editor of a "magazine night" (for which she solicited a contribution from MacMillan), as performer, reading papers and reciting poems, but she would never enter a debate. To a cousin—who described her as "a pert girl" at that time—she explained her choice of elocution as a device against being refuted in debate. Repeating someone else's words, she was safe from argument or error. But she told MacMillan, "I could not . . . 'speak' in public if I died for it . . . to get up and *say* anything—horrors, I should die on the spot . . . I just sit like a log while the others are talking eloquently. If I were to get up on my feet I wouldn't have an idea in my head. The worst of it is people won't believe I *can't*. They know I can write slickly and read well and they think that it is just sheer obstinacy that I won't speak in a discussion. But I simply *cannot*. I would stammer and and grope and make grammatical errors that would make the flesh creep on my bones in cold-blooded thought afterwards."

It was a "horror" she overcame in later years. But it may explain why pen-friendships meant so much to her. Here she could discuss calmly, rationally and without stress, and never fear painting herself into a syntactical corner.

At Cavendish she was still the pleasant, community-spirited Maud Montgomery they had always known, who looked after the flowers at Sunday services; church organist, dedicated Sunday School teacher, "a pert girl," a woman who "sat up stiffly," as she wrote of her attendance at a Sunday School convention, "dressed in my best and looked attentive," while "inwardly bored to tears." But at the end of 1908 the girl who had appeared "pert" to her cousin was writing about her "morbid brooding over certain worries and troubles that have been ever present in my life for the past six years. They are caused by people and circumstances over which I have no control, so I am quite helpless in regard to them. . . ." And increasingly she was finding that the narrowness of her moral training and religious upbringing had imprisoned her in a rigid morality against which her inner self rebelled, but from which she could not escape.

What would the good folk of Cavendish have thought, had they known their Sunday School teacher thought her class of half-grown girls "stupid and commonplace"? . . . "Yes, I teach a Sunday School class—but I don't like it much. . . . I have to follow the old traditional paths of thought & expression or I would get into hot water immediately." Would they have been shocked by the woman who was writing when she was thirty-two, "I don't think I have really any belief in any particular kind of a future life. I believe that there is life after death, that's all"? Or would they have been scandalized to know that she was wondering whether religion had been a curse or a blessing, and "*cannot* accept the *divinity* of Christ"?

Friends and neighbours of another writer once boasted: "*They* know you as you write. *We* know you as you are." Maud Montgomery might well have made the reply that came swiftly back: "You who live with me know me as I *seem*. They who *read* me know me as I am." Yet even her books do not reveal the full truth about this complex, deeply introspective woman. Her books bubble. "Nowadays my reviewers say that my forte is humour," she wrote in 1917. She had a sense of the ludicrous, a feeling for the juxtaposition of words that could make a phrase irresistibly comic, and often redeemed an unlucky leaning toward sentimental romance and purple prose.

"Mrs. Emily Frost . . . who . . . had yearned for the Apostle spoons, tried to look grateful for a bed which was too big for any of her tiny rooms . . . Joscelyn Dark got the claw-footed mahogany table Mrs Palmer Dark had hoped for, and Roger Dark got the Georgian candlesticks and Mrs Denzil's eternal hatred."

"Even Pat [the cat] had a ribbon of blue, which he clawed off and lost half an hour after it was tied on him. Pat did not care for vain adornments of the body."

But despite her sense of humour and her ready laughter, Maud was no sunny, effervescent Anne. Perhaps in her poems, one of the few vehicles that can carry the expression of deep feeling without embarrassment or pretentiousness—perhaps only in writing never meant for public reading—did she allow herself to lift the veil of conventional reticence. Many of those who thought they were intimate with her might have been surprised to discover the distance at which they stood in her private catalogue of intimates.

"I wish I'd never written about 'kindred spirits' in my book," she wrote savagely to Weber after *Anne of Green Gables* appeared. "Every freak who has written to me about it, claims to be a 'kindred spirit'. I'm going to dedicate my new book to 'kindred spirits'. *You*, therefore, will have a share in it. But many folks will *think* they have who *haven't*."

Years later, her younger son would recognize the loneliness in which she lived behind a facade of sociability. "She was extremely sensitive, although an excellent dissembler, and though she experienced great peaks, she also fell to great depths emotionally, which does not make for tranquillity. This rigidity and sensitivity prevented any easy camaraderie in the family, but she was capable of inspiring deep affection in all of us."

Maud was thirty-three when Anne of Green Gables *was published in June 1908.*

Old Prince of Wales College, Charlottetown

Maud's First Class teacher's certificate

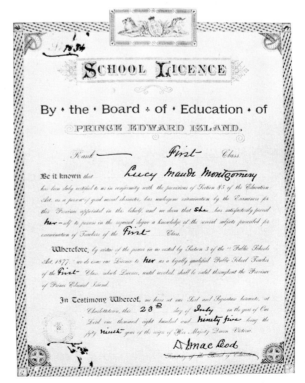

Anne of Green Gables.

Chapter 1.
Mrs. Rachel Lynde is Surprised.

Mrs. Rachel Lynde lived just where the Avonlea main road dipped down into a little hollow, "with a" traversed by a brook that had its source away back in the woods of the old Cuthbert place: it was reputed to be an intricate headlong brook in its earlier course through those woods, with dark secrets of pool and cascade. But by the time it reached Lynde's Hollow it was a quiet, well-conducted little stream, for not even a brook could run past Mrs. Rachel Lynde's door without due regard for decency and decorum; it probably was conscious that Mrs. Rachel was sitting at her window, keeping a sharp eye on everything that pa.
Note B.
and that if she noticed aught odd, or out of place, she would never rest in

Chapter 1, page 1: Maud begins Anne of Green Gables

*The Lake of Shining Waters lies below the Park Corner
home of Maud's Campbell cousins.*

Ephraim Weber, the first of Maud's two lifelong pen-friends

George MacMillan on holiday. MacMillan was a true "kindred spirit" to whom Maud could pour out her inmost thoughts and feelings. Begun in 1903, their correspondence continued right up to 1942, when Maud lay on her death bed.

George MacMillan in later years

The Reverend Ewan Macdonald had been Presbyterian pastor at Cavendish. He was forty, Maud thirty-six when they married in 1911.

The Campbell house at Park Corner, where L.M. Montgomery was married, 5 July 1911

The Reverend Ewan and Mrs. Macdonald at the Glasgow Exhibition during their honeymoon in 1911. Maud said he looked "fierce."

Ewan Macdonald and George Boyd MacMillan

Dollar Glen, near Alloa in Scotland. "One of the wildest, grandest spots we have seen," wrote Maud on her honeymoon.

CHAPTER ELEVEN

Child's-eye
view

All through these years, a little boy—her cousin Ken Mac-neill—was spending his summers at the farm, recreating (did she realize it?) her own joyous childhood and building up the same wonderful memories. He was also forming a child's-eye view of his cousin Maud, and in his seventies he took a nostalgic look at those years.

"I am afraid I did not ever attain what is now called a *rapport* with Maudie. She was not an outgoing woman, even though well educated and somewhat travelled. She had a small and narrow facial appearance and a somewhat small tight-lipped mouth ["I am a petite person with very delicate features," she once wrote of herself]. Instinctively at first I did not particularly like her, nor, I think, she me. She frequently sort of nipped at me, but I would guess that I was a little brat myself and very likely deserved her feelings about me. The relationship was not improved by two incidents in which I caused her some pain and embarrassment. For some unknown reason I cut off her pet cat's whiskers: and was caught looking at her from a cliff top perch, getting ready to go bathing in the Gulf which bordered our farm. It did not at the time endear Maud Montgomery to me, as she gave me a sort of rough time for a while about it. Eventually it was forgotten, and as I grew up, I think we had a mutual liking and admiration. At least I did not find her so hateful when I attended her Sunday School class later on, and she even sided with my grandmother against my mother on the problem of whether or not I was to be served tea—a privilege that in those days generally was extended at a later age. My mother went down to defeat and I had tea thereafter.

"The front portion of the home we lived in faced the out-door privy, favourably situated among the apple blossoms. That front entrance was little-used, except for excursions to the privy, as the family itself, everybody who came for the mail, all salespeople, and the peddlers who brought thread, pins, corkscrews, paper, pens, pencils and hard candy for me, used the back door, which faced on the road.

"When I got to be four or five and had some notion of the wonderful summers ahead of me, I could hardly wait until school got out and we started off—my father, a Presbyterian minister, my mother, pretty and fifteen years younger than he, and me. It was an all-day journey from Saint John, New Brunswick, to Shediac by rail, thence by steamer to Summerside, then a train again to Hunter River, the nearest railhead to Cavandish eleven long miles away. We were met there by my Uncle John with a two-seat buggy and room on the back for the trunk we lugged along with us, a most tiresome trip of nearly two hours. And then, finally, there was Grandma Macneill and Maudie, and a fine farm dinner with everything included. I had had nothing but a couple of sandwiches since breakfast, bought on the train.

"There were two homes on the Macneill farm—my Grand-mother's, and—about a hundred yards away—my Uncle John's, the only one of Grandma's children who did not seek his for-tune in other parts of the country. He stayed and ran the farm.

"The house was between two orchards, with lovely apple, cherry, and other fruits. Maud had her bedroom on the upper floor facing south, with an immense cherry tree for a view. Here she typed daily during my years, and at that time mostly poems, which she dutifully mailed off to magazines in both Canada and the United States. Such half-forgotten names as *Argosy, Smart Set* and *Everybody's* come to mind. From these publications she got back small checks, which seemed to my child's mind huge amounts running at times over $100, but mostly less than that."

The variety of publications whose defences Maud stormed —and often breached—show how assiduously she studied the markets of the day, scorning none, however small; nor giving up hope for any poem or story until all possible outlets had been tried. In mid-1907, a poem that had fruitlessly gone the rounds of every American magazine and finally been sent to *The Canadian Magazine* "to get rid of it" brought her an unexpected two dollars. She was not above producing to order what she called "sensational trash." She wrote about a commissioned serial, "I shall be ashamed of it but shall expect a liberal check," and was pleased with the eighty dollars it earned. She also, reluctantly, undertook hackwork, writing stories to fit pictures supplied by a Toronto magazine, *East and West*.

Weber got a triumphant listing in each letter of the "new mags." she had broken into, and the amount she had been paid. The information was, of course, of keen interest to him, looking as he still was for new publications that might accept his own work. He had returned from his unprofitable venture into full-time free-lance writing in Philadelphia, and was homesteading on the prairies again. In 1904, Maud had earned a total of $591.85: at the end of 1906 the year's total was more than seven hundred dollars. The acceptances were becoming more frequent, the amounts larger. December 1906 saw the sale of a five-thousand-word story to *Everybody's* for "*one hundred dollars. . . .* It had also been rejected twice," said Maud smugly, "once by a magazine that pays $30 per story and once by a magazine that pays *ten*."

Though writing was her major obsession, the daily round occupied more of her time. "She did her share of the housework, including cooking, dishwashing, cleaning and picking fruit for canning, the usual chores on any farm," says her cousin Ken. "I recall that candle making—tallow candles—was one of them. We did have kerosene lamps but we used candles to amplify these. There were no stores within some miles, so we had to depend for food and other supplies on itinerant peddlers. Of course my uncle grew all forms of vegetables, which we used or stored in our potato cellar. One thing I will never forget—the unalterable rule that I should be home by at least eight o'clock at night, and either Maud—or more likely Grandma—would mix up what seems in retrospect a horrible mixture, but which in fact I came to like, a mix of molasses and water. The Coca Cola of its day!"

There is no doubt that she was trapped in the position of the unmarried daughter on whom responsibility devolves for the care of an aged parent. Some days were especially trying. "I have been sizzling over a hot stove all the afternoon making lemon pies—for we have a houseful of company at present— and just getting madder all the time. Then I went out to water my garden and found that some mysterious grub is eating off all my verbenas. That turned my comparative into superlative and I was just *maddest*."

But there was an avenue of at least temporary escape. "I have fled up here to my den where the cares of garden and the deceitfulness of lemon pies cannot enter in. I have got my window wide open and a big jar of garden heliotrope on my table before me. It is mellowing my temper very quickly. I am drinking in its exquisite odor like a cup of aerial wine— and—and—dog-days will pass—and the lemon pies turned out very well—and I'm not over fond of verbenas anyhow and it's a pretty good old world after all!"

Until her grandmother's death released her, the years for Maud were a daily round of pleasure and boredom mixed, to which her writing had always to be subordinated. The summer visitors made extra work—"Uncle Leander and Aunt Mary and their son Kennedy have been here for two months," she wrote in 1909, and as the years went by and Uncle Leander became increasingly a nervous invalid, "his entertainment is a somewhat difficult matter"—but they also brought benefits. Maud loved to bathe, but needed a companion, as the shore was "rather lonely and infested by lobster fishermen." With her aunt she could go almost every evening. "Some of our dips were done in a heavy surf. It was the cream of bathing to stand there and let a wave break up around one's neck in a glorious smother of white foam." In 1904 she had written, "I'm trying to learn to swim and am getting on decently. I can waggle my arms all right and wiggle my legs just so but the trouble seems to be to wiggle and waggle them both together and between times I go ker-souse." She never did succeed. "It seems to me a perplexing business," she was writing two years later.

"Maudie used to go swimming with my mother," recalls

Ken—"I guess you'd call it bathing, they didn't swim, to my knowledge, and they confined this activity to where the rock cliffs ended and the sand beach began. The fabulous beach was called Cawnpore. I never got bored with it, even using it alone. I loved to swim there, and walk the sands, especially when there was a real old-fashioned nor'easter blowing up waves of six to eight feet high. Reading her work, I note that Maud was a little sea-struck, too. She seems to have had a feeling for the gulf and its ceaseless moods, as did I. I simply can't remember seeing her down there too often but maybe our visits just didn't coincide.

"I could watch the gulf shore for hours. The beach ends abruptly as if cut off by a huge knife, and instead of rolling sandhills and dunes, it turned into cliffs some twenty to thirty feet high, all red stone and a peculiar type of clay one could cut out and carve with a knife into various shapes. There was a road cut from the beach up to the field level, and this we used to haul up loads of seaweed to be stored and used for fertilizer. For this we had a little ground sled pulled by a horse. The rocky shore-front also produced treasures like mussels, which I used to pick off and cook over a little wood fire.

"Later I was recruited into the farm work and did my share of hoeing turnips, harvesting grain and hay, running the mower and rake (thrilling for a kid), and always fishing the brook—where as well as swimming I made little dams and water-wheels—the lake and the Gulf of St Lawrence for mackerel and cod."

Maud's greatest pleasure was her garden. Her letters to both Weber and MacMillan are strung with whimsical expressions of her joy in flowers. *Oh, I hope heaven will be all flowers. One could be good if one lived in a lily. . . . I've known roses I expect to meet in heaven. . . . I hope next time I'm born I'll be a Madonna lily. . . . My sweet-peas are lovely —I think they must be the souls of good butterflies. . . . I have a lovely 'mum out—seven or eight great fluffy pale pink flowers out on it. The 'mum is a society lady, all frills and chiffons and languid grace. . . .* Still—"wouldn't you rather be a rose for a fortnight than a 'mum forever?"

Gardening was also one of MacMillan's passions, and both

ways across the Atlantic went bulbs, cuttings, seeds, pressed flowers, received on each side with rapturous expressions of gratitude. MacMillan's gifts over the years, especially books, were carefully chosen to cater to Maud's special interests. "I think you come the nearest of anybody I know to 'inspiration' in choosing your Xmas gifts with regard to the recipient's taste," Maud commented. He sent her Flora Klickmann's *Flower Patch* books, Emily Handasyde Buchanan's *The Four Gardens*, Frances Hodgson Burnett's *The Secret Garden, Down the Garden Path* by Beverley Nichols; and for other pleasures, other books: Kenneth Grahame's *The Golden Age* and *Dream Days* and *The Wind in the Willows*; David Grayson's *The Friendly Road*. He sent her calendars each year, and bundles of magazines—the *Westminster Gazette, John o' London's*, and when her boys were young, the *Children's Newspaper*, as well as stamps and crests for their collections.

Her own gifts to him were selected with equal care, often North American books he might not otherwise have encountered: poems by Marjorie Pickthall, Sir Charles G. D. Roberts, Bliss Carman, Robert Service; works by Frederick Philip Grove, Oliver Wendell Holmes, Jack London, Ernest Thompson Seton; later, the prize-winning novels of Martha Ostenso and Mazo de la Roche.

From MacMillan, too, came boxes of the souvenirs they both cherished—shells, bits of rock, a piece of the stone from Blarney Castle, the little fossils from Holy Island known as St. Cuthbert's beads. "A certain good man here [the Customs Officer] thinks me a lunatic and probably has the same opinion of you," cried Maud. . . . "He eyed me askance as I opened it and I know I forfeited his good opinion forever by my rapture over its contents. What sane woman . . . could attach any value to such trash and what idiot had sent them all the way from Scotland!"

Did she like music?—MacMillan had asked. Yes, very much. But—"*Color* is to me what music is to some. Everybody *likes* color: with me it is a passion. I revel in it. . . . Everything you say of music I can say of color. . . . On my table is a color effect of yellow California poppies that makes me dizzy with delight every time I look at it." At a recent vaudeville performance she had seen a Rainbow Dance—"a combination of colored lights thrown on a white-clad girl dancing. I never saw or imagined anything so utterly beautiful and *satisfying*. My emotions were exactly what you describe yours as being when listening to music." It was Maud's love of colour that sometimes loaded her work with an excess of ecstatic adjectives.

Letters went on crossing the Atlantic, crossing Canada: ten, twelve, twenty pages of gossip, of philosophical and literary exchanges, discussions of "soul mates," the power of dreams, extrasensory perception, Keats, Kipling and kittens, the disservice done to religion by austere puritanical interpretations. In an April 1907 letter to MacMillan, Maud touched on a subject that would take a firm hold of her mind in later years. "Do you believe such things—'premonitions', I mean? I *don't* and *yet*—well, strange things do certainly happen. I never had any presentiments myself that worked out to anything, although I've had scores that didn't. But I've known odd things in this line." In later years, tormented by the horrors of the war in Europe, she would interpret her nightmares in the light of current events, proving their validity to her own satisfaction. But true premonition (if there be such a thing) eluded her. Meeting a young Island friend shortly before she was drowned, Maud remembered afterwards that she had had "no shattering 'second sight'" to forewarn her of the tragedy.

But, like a child returning again and again to touch, fascinated, a bright forbidden jewel, Maud would hover all her life at the edge of the occult, convincing herself finally that some of her dreams at least were predictive. *I don't believe . . . . but I want to believe and I half believe*: this was the way her thoughts led her, although she was quick to mock herself for credulity. She listed to MacMillan the coincidences that impressed her when some random comment in a letter was followed by the same word or thought in an article or conversation. Telepathy, transmigration and—most of all— reincarnation caught her imagination and offered a reason for hope that the beloved dead might not be gone forever, that known familiar beauties might not be lost in death, that somewhere there was *more*. "How could you and I know each other so well," she marvelled to MacMillan in 1936, "when we have met in person only once and very briefly, if we had not *recognized* some old friend of a former existence—perhaps in this planet, perhaps in one circling round Sirius?"

CHAPTER TWELVE

Anne of
Green Gables

"We are just in the middle of housecleaning!" Maud wrote to Weber on May 2, 1907. ". . . For the past four days I've been scrubbing and whitewashing and digging out old corners and I feel as if all the dust I've stirred up and swept out and washed off has got into my soul and settled there and will remain there forever, making it hopelessly black and grimy and unwholesome. Of course I *know* it won't but knowing is such a different thing from *believing*. . . .

"I wonder if it's absolutely necessary to houseclean? I wonder if nine-tenths of the things we think so necessary really are so! But I shall go on housecleaning and wondering! I may have given up belief in fore-ordination and election and the Virgin Birth; *but* I have not and never shall be guilty of the heresy of asserting that it is not vital to existence that the house should be torn up once a year and scrubbed!"

This letter, however, had other and truly momentous news. "Well, last fall and winter I went to work and wrote a *book*. I didn't squeak a word to anyone about it because I feared desperately I wouldn't find a publisher for it. When I got it finished and typewritten I sent it to the L. C. Page Co. of Boston and a fortnight ago, after two months of suspense I got a letter from them accepting my book and offering to publish it on the 10-per cent royalty basis!"

From Boston had come an austere but encouraging letter to Dear Madam, written on April 8:

"We take pleasure in advising you that our readers report favorably with regard to your girls' story 'Anne of Green

Gables', and if mutually satisfactory arrangements can be made, we shall be glad to add the book to our next season's list.

"Will you kindly advise whether you desire to sell the manuscript outright, or whether you wish it published on a moderate royalty basis, in the former case advising us of the amount you wish to receive.

"We shall be glad also to hear of your plans with regard to future writing, and take the liberty of suggesting that if you are not otherwise at work, it might be a good idea to write a second story dealing with the same character."

The item from her notebook of ideas that had been the hook on which Maud hung her story was a simple two-line entry: *Elderly couple apply to orphan asylum for a boy. By mistake a girl is sent them.* A slight enough theme, but Maud enriched the central idea with an abundance of anecdotal detail and a host of characters shrewdly observed and presented with verve and an amused tolerance for human frailties. The link was the radiant, volatile child who ran like quicksilver through the fictional community of Avonlea.

Maud had not, in fact, actually written the book in the fall and winter of 1906-07. What she had done was revise and expand and recopy an earlier story begun in the spring of 1904, completed by October 1905, and five times sent hopefully out to publishers. From four of them it had returned with nothing more than a printed rejection slip: the fifth commented that readers had found some merit in the story, "but not enough to warrant its acceptance." The disheartened author tossed the manuscript away "in an old hatbox in the clothes room". When time allowed, she planned to cut the story back to its original seven chapters, and assure herself of thirty or possibly forty dollars from its sale as a serial.

But rummaging a year later and discovering the half-forgotten manuscript, Maud "began turning over the leaves, reading a bit here and there. It didn't seem so very bad."

Her old second-hand typewriter bought in 1901 "never made the capitals plain and wouldn't print 'm's' at all." In June 1906 she had invested in a better one—second-hand still, but newer than her former one, and with the standard keyboard the other one had lacked. Typing the revised manu-script was a slow job while she learned the position of the keys. Her writing pattern, she confided to Weber, was three hours snatched from other duties—two hours for writing and one for typing; after her success in selling *Anne*, she kept an hour in the morning for magazine work, an hour in the after-noon for typing, and an hour in the evening for books. "Can you compose on the machine?" she had asked MacMillan. "I cannot do so at all. I have to write everything out by pen first and then copy it."

A year dragged by before Anne made her public appear-ance. Maud was pleased by her success in finding a publisher, but she had had no illusions about her book. "Don't stick up your ears now," she told Weber, "imagining that the great Canadian novel has been written at last. It is merely a juvenil-ish story, ostensibly for girls. . . . I did not dream it would be the success it was. I thought girls in their teens might like it but that was the only audience I hoped to reach." By early March 1908 she had sent back the last of the proofs and expected the book to be out within days. Meanwhile she went on shooting her arrows—short stories, serials and poems: some of them hit the target, some did not.

She was well into the sequel the publishers had suggested, though she found it heavy going in an unusually hot summer, not flowing as spontaneously as the first book had done. She was wrangling with the Page Company, she told MacMillan, over her byline. "I want it published under the name 'L. M. Montgomery' as all my work has been. The Page Co. insist on 'Lucy Maud Montgomery' which I loathe. Don't know who will come out on top, probably the publishers."

But they didn't. At last, in June 1908, *Anne* was launched, and an astounded L. M. Montgomery began to understand that she had produced a best seller. "Anne seems to have hit the public taste." By mid-September the book had gone through four editions, by the end of November through six—"and that must mean a decent check when payday comes." By May 1909 *Anne* was in her fifth English edition, and Mac-Millan was sending her the reviews.

A clipping service provided her with the reviews that came

pouring in from all over North America: at summer's end, Maud had received sixty. "Two were harsh, one contemptuous, two mixed praise with blame and the remaining fifty-five were kind and flattering beyond my highest expectations." Though she would complain in later years that "the only papers who ever give me bad slams are Canadian ones," Maud could hardly find fault with the Montreal *Herald*'s "A book which will appeal to the whole English speaking world—one of the most attractive figures Canadian fiction has produced." Or of the Montreal *Star*'s "The most fascinating book of the season." Or even of her own province's verdict, the Charlottetown *Daily Patriot*'s full column of praise for "the first novel of Miss Lucy Maud Montgomery, who is well known to our readers as a writer of charming verse . . . 'Anne of Green Gables' will appeal to only three classes of readers, those who have imagination, those who have some sense of that rarest of qualities, humor, and those who have not allowed themselves to grow old or to forget that once upon a time they were children. . . . The characters are drawn well and with restraint. . . . The book . . . has running through it a delicate vein of humor; the description of nature throughout is that of a keenly-observant and equally keenly-appreciative lover of the woods and fields and skies. . . ."

Though the New York *Times* said "Anne is a bore," and considered her "a mawkish, tiresome, impossible heroine," the American press outvoted its reviewer. The Pittsburgh *Chronicle* thought Anne "one of the cleverest creations in recent fiction." The Milwaukee *Free Press* remarked "the elusive charm of personality. She is full of flavour." The New York *American* found it "an idyllic story, one of the most delightful books we have read for many a day." And— accolade of accolades—the venerable, seventy-three-year-old Mark Twain sent a personal letter to Maud. "He wrote me that in *Anne* I had created 'the dearest, and most lovable child in fiction since the immortal Alice'. Do you think I wasn't *proud* of Mark's encomium? Oh, perhaps not!"

She could not complain of the publicity the Page Company gave to her work. Only a month after the publication of *Anne* an incident had occurred that Page turned to good account. "A big party of Orangemen were going on a picnic. At the Boston North St. station, they saw a copy of *Anne of Green Gables* bound in green on a newsstand. They took, or pretended to take—they were likely half drunk—the title as a personal insult, marched across to the Page building, the band playing horrible dirges, and nearly mobbed the place. One of the editors came out and told them that although the title might be offensive, 'the heroine, Anne, had hair of a distinct orange hue.' Thereupon they 'adopted' Anne as their mascot, gave her three cheers and went on their way rejoicing." Enterprising Page spread the story in the press from coast to coast, as well as producing posters and booklets to advertise *Anne*.

In the first five years of publication by Page, *Anne* ran through thirty-two editions. The thirty-eighth edition, in May 1914, was a "Popular Impression" limited to 150,000 copies.

In the first three years of publication in England (by Sir Isaac Pitman) *Anne* sold nine thousand copies: but by 1919, the first four titles that followed in the *Anne* series were out of print. From 1921 to 1933, eight of Maud's later books were published by Hodder and Stoughton, and more than a hundred thousand of these were sold.

In 1925, when the *Anne* books had been out of print for some six years, George G. Harrap & Co. Ltd. in England and Angus and Robertson, Ltd. in Australia contracted with the Page Company of Boston to publish them again in a uniform edition, and all the old interest was at once revived. Harrap also published Maud's four last books in 1935, 1936, 1937 and 1939.

In 1956, three million copies of Montgomery novels were circulating in British countries (excluding Canada), and *Anne of Green Gables* accounted for six hundred thousand of these. Since that date, about a quarter of a million copies of the *Anne* and *Avonlea* books have been sold in Britain. *Anne* has been published in more than fifteen languages, including French, Spanish, Italian, Dutch, Finnish, Swedish, Norwegian, Danish, Polish, Japanese, Icelandic and (in English) Braille.

Were she living today, Maud might well marvel, as she was often to do, that this creature of her imagination could live on so vividly through all the years since 1908. She would see Anne in two movies—silent and talking—and in two plays. In 1929 she would hear from a Dutch fan—a missionary teacher in Java—about the performance of *Anne of Green Gables* in a private school for the daughters of wealthy Mohammedan families; and she would be charmed by the accompanying photograph showing the little Javanese faces of the children portraying her sturdy Prince Edward Island characters, Matthew in top hat and swallow-tailed coat.

In 1965, *Anne* moved on to greater triumphs. In that year "a completely Canadian summer festival" was launched to run through July and August in Charlottetown, and has since become what someone has called "the nation's leading showcase for original musical theatre." In the 946-seat theatre of the city's Confederation Centre, opened the year before as a memorial to the Fathers of Confederation, *Anne of Green Gables* was the star attraction—a musical based on Maud's book, written and composed by Donald Harron and Norman Campbell. It was a tremendous success from its first performance and followed its Charlottetown triumph with a sell-out cross-Canada tour in 1967. The Charlottetown company took it to Osaka for two weeks of sold-out performances during Expo 70 and for a two-week Christmas session in New York in 1971. With a company that included three of the Charlottetown cast, with Barbara Hamilton as Marilla, it ran from March 1969 to January 1970 for a highly popular London run. An African production opened in Nairobi at the end of 1969.

And the interest continues. Anne has long been a Japanese favourite; a part of *Anne of Green Gables* is included in one of the junior secondary school Japanese language textbooks. Of the one hundred and fifty Japanese girls interviewed for positions as guides at the Canadian Pavilion for Expo 70, one hundred and forty-nine had either read the book or knew the story. Since 1954, when the Shinco Company began publishing Montgomery books in paperback in Japan (there are sixteen titles in print today), about seven million copies have been sold.

In January 1972 *Anne* was adapted for television by Julia Jones, and shown by BBC-1 in Britain in five episodes, repeated eighteen months later. A sequel based on *Anne of Avonlea* and *Anne of the Island* followed early in 1975.

But in 1908, that was for the future. One has to fall back on the cliché. In 1908, how little could Maud know, as she tried to cope with the immediate overwhelming response to the book, that this response would show few signs of diminishing nearly seventy years later. "I have never, until recently, ever read Anne of Green Gables," confessed her amused cousin Ken, "though Anne was literally written over my head in the room above while I was lulled to sleep to the tune of a tapping typewriter. I was a small boy and nothing could be more beneath me than to read a girl's book, no matter how good. But you know, I really like it. And reading Maudie's own story of her childhood years later, I have come to the conclusion that in certain respects little girls are much like little boys in their imaginations and their fears and embarrassments."

Maud herself had noted certain similarities. When MacMillan asked whether she thought men or women recovered more quickly from an unhappy love affair, she replied: "Well, I don't think it is a matter of *sex* at all, but instead of temperament and individual . . . the difference is mostly [one] of circumstance not of sex. I really think that men and women are much more alike than commonly supposed."

CHAPTER THIRTEEN

Delights and
disappointments

The first royalty cheque, for seventeen hundred and thirty dollars, arrived in February 1909. This represented nine cents of the ninety-cent wholesale price of the book: the retail price was $1.50.

Naturally enough, the reviews had pleased Maud, but something was missing. "One thing surprises me in the reviews and one thing disappoints me," she complained to MacMillan. "I am surprised that they seem to take the book so seriously—as if it were meant for grown-up readers and not merely for girls. The disappointment comes in this:—I had hoped to learn something from the reviews. I knew that the book must have faults which its author could not perceive, and I expected the reviews to point them out. But there is no agreement. What one critic praises as the most attractive feature in the book another condemns as its greatest fault— and there am I, no wiser than before."

By the end of her career she had learned to expect no help from critics. "I gave up trying to fathom the mentality of reviewers years ago. My literary scrapbooks of thirty years make very amusing reading now. They are a series of contradictions."

Despite the heady wine of success, Maud found herself restless and ill at ease. Tourists were demanding to meet her and "I don't want to be met." She resented newspaper publicity about her private life. "I don't care what they do about my book—*it* is public property—but I wish they would leave my *ego* alone," she wrote to MacMillan. To Weber, when he half-humorously suggested that he might write her life if

76

she predeceased him, she wrote: "No, you won't! Nobody shall. I'd haunt you if you did. Biography is a *screaming farce*. No man or woman was ever truly depicted. Biographies, even the best, are one—or at the most two-sided—and every human being has half a dozen different sides. . . . And I know I wouldn't want some of *my* soul moods depicted—no, nor any of them—for the evil ones would shame me and the good ones would be desecrated by revelation."

Yet she was an avid reader of biographies, and in later years she modified her attitude, giving consent to an article Weber proposed to submit: adding, however, "If I were dead you'd have a better chance!"

She was not physically well, suffering continual headaches, lack of appetite, and weariness, she said, of body, soul and spirit. "We had a houseful of guests all summer"—Uncle Leander and his wife, and cousin Ken again?—"the weather was fearfully hot and I was very much worried in one way or another almost constantly." As well, she was discovering unsuspected jealousies and unfriendliness. "If you want to find out just how much *envy* and *petty spite* and *meanness* exists in people, even people who call themselves your friends, just write a successful book or do something they can't do, and you'll find out!" she told Weber in September, less than three months after *Anne* had appeared. ". . . A certain class of people will take it as a personal insult to themselves, will belittle you and your accomplishment in every way and will go out of their way to make sure that you are informed of their opinions." In December she was still smarting. "I could not begin to tell you all the petty flings of malice and spite of which I have been the target of late, even among some of my own relations."

Many years later, when neighbours were priding themselves on their early friendship with the now famous author, Maud wrote ironically to MacMillan of basing one of her most hateful characters on a woman who had posed to a journalist "as my early friend and helper." She did not spare the journalist either. "I was never in my life called 'Lucy Maud'. My friends called me 'Maud' and nothing else."

She was still sending out stories and poems, cannily "peddling off my old MSS," some of which she was honest enough to recognize had sold only because of her new-made fame. She was also honest enough to recognize faults in *Anne*. The ending was too conventional (but then, how did she know she was going to have to write a sequel, she asked?). Anne's success at school was too good for literary art. "I suppose she's all right but I'm so horribly tired of her that I can't see a single merit in her or the book and can't really convince myself that people are sincere when they praise her."

Nevertheless, she completed her sequel, *Anne of Avonlea,* taking Anne through two years as a teacher, and sent it off to Page early in November 1908, though it was not published until the following September to avoid providing a "rival" while the first book was still selling well. Maud felt that the new book lacked freshness, and she feared that "if the thing takes, they'll want me to write her through college. The idea makes me sick. I feel like the magician in the Eastern story who became the slave of the 'jinn' he had conjured out of a bottle. If I'm to be dragged at Anne's chariot wheels the rest of my life," she concluded in a fine flurry of mixed metaphor, "I'll bitterly repent having 'created' her."

Her fears were only too well justified. Her *Anne* books would bring her fame and fortune (though not as much of the latter as she should have earned, owing to holes—unapparent at the time—in her contract), and she dutifully produced a new one each time her publisher requested it. The writing was to prove a labour and Anne a torment as random gaps in her life were successively filled. "That detestable Anne," she was writing, only a month after the second *Anne* book was finished. In 1915 she plodded restlessly through *Anne of the Island* (Anne in college), published in July, unable to do what she thought of as "real" work because of the war. *Anne's House of Dreams* (her first years of marriage) came out in August 1917. At the end of 1919 Maud completed *Rainbow Valley* (Anne's children growing up) and began work on her tenth work of fiction, *Rilla of Ingleside.* "Then I hope to say farewell to Anne forever." The book, completed in 1920, was to be "positively the last of the Anne series. I have gone completely 'stale' on Anne and *must* get a new heroine. Six books are enough to write about any girl."

The story of Rilla, Anne's youngest daughter, was set in wartime years, and Maud meant it as "a tribute to the girlhood of Canada," she wrote, though she dedicated it in a moment of great personal loss to a dearly loved and recently dead cousin, Frederica Campbell MacFarlane. It was, she said, her only novel written with a purpose. "In it I definitely and for all time conclude the Anne series, I swear it by the nine gods of Clusium." It was delightful to be rid of Anne, "who weighed on me like an incubus when she ceased to be an inspiration."

Yet in July 1936, obediently but "unwillingly," she began work on *Anne of Windy Poplars*, taking Anne back to the days before her marriage when she was writing love letters to Gilbert Blythe. And in 1938 she crammed a "pot-boiler" into four months of writing, published the following year as *Anne of Ingleside*, when Anne's children were in their baby days. That the series was not written in the chronological order of Anne's life probably added to Maud's weary revulsion from each successive task.

She was kept busy explaining that no, *this* particular character was not a portrait of *that* real person. "You can't describe people *exactly* as they are. The *details* would be true, the *tout ensemble* utterly false. I have been told my characters are marvellously 'true to life'—nay, Cavendish readers have got them all fitted to real Cavendish people. Yet there isn't a portrait in the book. They are all 'composites.' "

To her cousin Murray Macneill, professor of mathematics at Dalhousie College, Halifax, and much older brother of Ken, she wrote in July 1909: "I was much pleased to receive your kind letter about my book and am glad to know you liked it. It has been a great surprise to me that Anne should have taken so well with 'grown-ups'. When I wrote it I thought it would be an amusing and harmless little tale for Sunday School libraries and 'kiddies', but I did not suppose it would appeal to older readers.

"However, it seems to have done so and I have received a great many kind letters about it, both from old acquaintances and strangers.

"My second Anne book will be out in September. . . . It will not be as successful as the first. I wrote it, not because I wanted to but because my publisher insisted and I do not think such 'made to order' books ever have much life in them."

She had felt no better at the end of December 1908 than when she wrote to Weber in September, despite a six-week rest from her writing. "Indeed, I think I would have been better at work. I had only more time for morbid brooding. . . ."

Had she resented the call of duty that had brought her back to Cavendish? "The past six years" for which unnamed worries and troubles had bothered her went back to 1902 and her departure from Halifax. She did no more than hint at the existence of or reason for her worries: but she continued to be out of sorts for the rest of the winter, and the "great depths" into which her son would see her fall from time to time in the years to come were a tremendous drain on her spirits at this time, a period when she should have been floating on airy clouds of joy. "I have not been especially well this winter," she wrote to Weber in March 1909. " . . . I've been very nervous and at times somewhat morbid. The doctor says my nervous system is run down. . . ."

Later in the same letter, in a discussion of Christian Science, she confessed that without any expectation of success, she had in the previous November "decided to try to cure myself of sick headaches from which I had suffered every few weeks for eight years." To her surprise, after repeating "Remove the cause of my headaches" several times, an imperious order to some unknown authority, the trouble suddenly cleared up. "I really hadn't the least faith in it. But it is a simple fact that I have never had a headache since I began! I discontinued the 'treatment' after a month but there has been no return of the headaches. I am not *altogether* convinced—it is possibly only a coincidence and they might have stopped anyhow. But I am 'almost persuaded' that it was the mental suggestion which did it. Anyhow 'faith' had nothing to do with it, for I had none."

Cured the headaches may have been, but the "treatment" did not work on what she called her "nervous trouble." Whatever ailed her this year had been caused by more than physical illness.

Perhaps the greatest blow to Maud's morale at this time was the unexpected death in January 1909 of her favourite great-aunt, Aunt Mary Lawson, whose prodigious memory and racy anecdotal talent were the source of so many incidents in Maud's books. She had been "a sort of second mother to me, a sweet, fine, plucky little woman who had lived a more truly heroic life than many of the heroes and heroines of history . . . I felt her death bitterly."

She was a bit more cheerful in September. The summer had been as busy as ever, with "a houseful of company." In the fall, she had had two pleasures. The second *Anne* book came out—though she "took this one very coolly and it caused merely a momentary ripple on the day's surface"—and she had started work on a new book with a new heroine, Sara Stanley. "It's to be called *The Story Girl* and I have the first sentence and the last paragraph written!" Published in May 1911, it would always be Maud's favourite: she thought of it as being more "literary" than *Anne*, a step on the way toward the "mature" books she still hoped to write.

Before *The Story Girl* appeared, her publishers had cashed in on her reputation by producing *Kilmeny of the Orchard*, based on an already published serial, *Una of the Garden*. Reviewers were right when they detected a warmed-over flavour in this fairy tale, with its contrived plot and Garden-of-Eden environment. Maud curled her lips over the comment that the book showed "the insidious influence of popularity and success": she "found it interesting" when Page reprinted it in the mid-1920s, but "it seemed as if somebody else had written it." Yet, though not literally true, the reviewers' criticism had been valid. No character in the book has any of the spicy realism with which Maud could so liberally pepper her pages and in which she gave the truest demonstration of her talent. "You speak of my having *three* styles," she replied to a perceptive MacMillan in May 1909. "I daresay that is true. But the style of Anne is my *real* style. The others are only skilfully assumed garments to suit the particular story being 'built'. I wrote Anne in my *own* style, and I think that is the secret of her success."

She had thankfully turned down an invitation to read a paper at a World's Congress of Women held in Toronto (an activity she would learn to enjoy in later years), though she would have liked to attend the conference for its "broadening influence." She felt similarly deprived by missing the performance of an *Island Hymn* she had written. The composer had been able to respond to curtain calls, but "the author couldn't go. She had to stay home and wish she could."

CHAPTER FOURTEEN

The wider world

But relief was on the way, together with some of the fruits of success. In September 1910 a telegram came from the Governor General, Earl Grey, who was to visit Charlottetown "and wishes to meet the author of 'Anne.'" There followed much scurrying around to get suitable dresses. Maud always enjoyed new dresses. All her early photographs show a girl and woman who liked pretty things, who cared about being neat and attractive, and her earnings had become more than adequate to allow indulgence in this pleasure. "I'm having a dream of a dress built for the occasion," she wrote to Mac-Millan once when she was to be a bridesmaid—"all white organdy and silk lace; made up with frills and puffs and shir-rings galore; and I'm to carry white carnations and asparagus fern and have lovely little high heeled white satin slippers."

She was delighted with her viceregal experience. She presented Earl Grey, at his request, with autographed copies of her books to date, and got along famously with the "tall, genial, elderly man with a frank, pleasant face and a most un-affected 'homely' manner" and his agreeable family at two dinners, one of them a formal state affair on board the yacht *Earl Grey*—"curtseying backward out of the 'presence' and all that. I narrowly escaped coming to grief over my train."

The *Examiner* included Maud's name in the list of persons accompanying the viceregal party, but the *Daily Patriot* gave her four and a quarter column inches as one whose books the Governor General "has read with much enjoyment. He informed the talented writer that her works were being received with much acceptance in the Old Country." The report mentioned Maud's latest work, *The Story Girl*, not to appear as a book until the following summer, but already receiving bids for magazine serialization.

In *The Story Girl*, Maud had been able to introduce many family and local legends. Though the child-characters were, she said, purely imaginary, no author can fail to draw his material from the whole gamut of previous experience: and many a child from Maud's schooldays, from the classrooms where she taught, from the neighbouring homes, must have contributed a habit, a mannerism, an idiosyncrasy, a physical feature, to the seven youngsters who clustered around Sara Stanley to hear of mysteries and ghosts and star-crossed loves. The original of the old blue chest sat in Uncle John Campbell's Park Corner home. The ghostly bell in an empty house was the newly repaired clock that had raised goose-pimples on Maud and Well and Dave. Peg Bowen was queer Mag Laird, the harmless witch-like creature wandering Island lanes and scaring the three eight-year-olds half to death. The story of Nancy and Betty Sherman featured Maud's own great-grandfather, Donald Montgomery, father of the Senator: and Margaret, whose heart had died with the captain of the *Fanny*, was living and beautiful still, when *The Story Girl* appeared.

The children's chatter is often funny and perceptive, and their characters are neatly differentiated, but the thread on which the story is strung is a frail one, and there is little to move the action forward or to invite continued interest except a gentle pleasure in the mood and setting. Anne and Emily both carry the reader on to new discoveries about developing personalities and life stories, and arouse a desire to learn what happens next. One becomes involved with Anne and Emily as one does not with Sara Stanley and her circle. These children have no passionate problems, no hearts bursting with love and hate and frustration.

In November 1910, Maud was invited to visit Boston, where she was a guest for two weeks at the home of Mr and Mrs L. C. Page, a bit awestruck by her welcome and by life in a big city, entertained at luncheons and dinners by literary and patriotic clubs and delighting all believers in womanliness and modesty. "I lived more, learned more, and enjoyed more in those fourteen days than I had done in the previous fourteen years." She spent a day in the Museum of Fine Arts "and wanted to spend a month." She visited the homes of Emerson, Hawthorne, Thoreau and the Alcotts, and was amused by a placard on a tumble-down house on the Concord road: "This is the original house Paul Revere *would* have stopped at if he had ever ridden this way."

A reception was held in her honour by the Boston Authors Club and in the library of the Page home she was interviewed by a reporter from the Boston *Republic*.

"Miss Montgomery is short and slight, indeed of a form almost childishly small, with delicate aquiline features, bluish-grey eyes and an abundance of dark brown hair. Her pretty pink evening gown somewhat accentuated her frail and youthful aspect.

"It would be easy to exaggerate the retiring manner and untouched simplicity of this already famous woman; nor was it easy to induce her to talk about herself and her books. Her attitude was clearly of extreme surprise at the success of the latter and the interest of the Bostonians in their author."

Yes, Boston was the first big city she had visited. Yes, she would like to travel, but it was clear that her heart was in her Island. Yes, "the background [of *Anne*] is real, the 'haunted wood' is real, the little girl and her chums are leaves out of other lives, and yes, I used to name the places that I especially loved, just as Anne did . . . but except for that there is nothing of autobiography in the book." No, she did not want to do a book about Anne's love story. "I want to leave 'Anne' just as she is forever; in her girlhood."

In the ensuing discussion of women's work and ideals, Miss Montgomery was revealed as "distinctly conservative. . . . For all her gentleness and marked feminity of aspect and sympathies, she impressed [this] writer as of determined character, with positive convictions on the advantage of the secluded country life with its opportunities for long reflection and earnest study. . . . She has no favour for woman suffrage; she believes in the home-loving woman; we could not imagine her as 'a woman of affairs', or aught"—wrote the reporter in a gush of sentimentality—"but the quiet little gentlewoman of the warm heart and the vigorous, creative brain that she is."

The quiet little gentlewoman was, however, much less demure, much more emphatic a personality than she seemed. "Maud could put up, and keep up, a front," says cousin Ken, his pre-adolescent wisdom not far off her son's later judgment of his mother's power of dissimulation. Could her Boston interviewer have seen a letter she had written to Weber a year earlier, he might have had second thoughts. Maud may have had "very little interest" in the specific matter of woman suffrage, but she had views about independence of choice for women and a right to speak for herself. "As for the woman suffrage question, I feel very little interest in it," she had stated, continuing rather contradictorily, "but I do believe that a woman with property of her own should have a voice in making the laws. Am I not as intelligent and capable of voting for my country's good as the Frenchman who chops my wood for me, and who may be able to tell his right hand from his left, but cannot read or write?

"So you wish 'married women everywhere were real companions to their husbands,' " she went on in her feminist mood. "So do I—as heartily as I wish that married men everywhere were real companions for their wives. You can't, as Emerson says, cut this matter off with only one side. It has to have two. As for 'spheres' [today Maud might have used the word 'roles'], I believe anyone's sphere—whether man or woman—is where they can be happiest and do the best work. The majority of women are happiest and best placed at home, just as the majority of men are in the world." (What hackles Maud would raise today by the implication that male occupations are in "the world" and women's are not!) She went on: "But there are exceptions to *both*. Some women are born for a public career, just as some men are *born* to *cook in a restaurant*. Yes, they are! Sex seems to me to enter very little into the question. There is no sex in mind, I do believe, and—'let each one find his own,' and her own, in business as well as matrimony."

Her former professor, Archibald MacMechan, has recalled that Maud was "gratefully remembered for a clever article on the education of women contributed to a 'Dalhousie number' of a local paper" in Halifax. "It is not a very long time, as time goes in the world's history," said Maud in the *Halifax Herald* of April 29, 1896, "since the idea of educating a girl beyond her 'three r's' would have been greeted with up lifted hands and shocked countenances. . . . Could she dream of opposing her weak feminine mind to the mighty masculine intellect which had been dominating the world of knowledge from a date long preceding the time when Hypatia was torn to pieces by the mob of Alexandria?

" 'Never,' was the approved answer. Girls . . . were taught reading and writing and a small smattering of foreign languages; they 'took' music and were trained to warble pretty little songs and instructed in the mysteries of embroidery and drawing. . . . The larger proportion of them, of course, married. . . . But there was always a certain number of unfortunates—let us call them so since they would persist in using the term—left to braid St Catherine's tresses for the term of their natural lives; and a hard lot truly was theirs in the past. If they did not live in meek dependence with some compassionate relative, eating the bitter bread of unappreciated drudgery, it was because they could earn a meagre and precarious subsistance in the few and underpaid occupations then open to women. . . . Their education had not fitted them to cope with any and every destiny. . . .

"But nowadays . . . a girl is no longer shut out from the Temple of Knowledge simply because she is a girl; she can compete, and has competed successfully with her brother in all his classes. . . ."

Maud went on to list the achievements of some women graduates in England, and proudly complimented Dalhousie College on never having barred women students. Since the first two women enrolled in 1881, "a goodly number" had graduated and been a credit to their Alma Mater. This year there were about fifty-eight female students, the largest number so far, and Maud was sure "that, in the years to come, the number will be very much larger." But she thought it unlikely that "girl students at Dalhousie, or at any other co-educational university, will be equal to the number of men."

In a limited way, Maud was one of the early feminists, setting out to earn her own living as a reporter in the early 1900s, and she was certainly one of Canada's earliest successful freelance writers, long before she produced her unexpected best seller. She made brave sounds, this independent, semi-feminist Maud. But she still considered the Victorian wife-and-mother ideal as the first and most important role for a woman, and saw education as a personal enrichment within the happier state of marriage, or at least something to fall back on if she remained single.

"The larger proportion of them, of course, married," she wrote of the earlier women, those who had not been educationally emancipated, "and we are quite ready to admit that they made none the poorer wives and mothers because they could not conjugate a Greek verb or demonstrate a proposition in Euclid. . . ." But Maud Montgomery could never have been totally happy merely as the "home-loving" woman her Boston interviewer saw, even had her own marriage been happy and satisfying, if she had not had her escape door in her writing and the fame it brought her.

In July 1909, Maud had told her cousin Murray Macneill that "Grandma had a real sick spell in May." Her grandmother was then nearing the age of eighty-five. She would live until March 10, 1911.

" . . . The most sorrowful period of my life," Maud wrote to MacMillan . . . "On March 5th my dear old grandmother, who has been the only mother I knew, became ill with pneumonia and five days later passed peacefully away. . . . I knew I could not hope to have her with me very much longer. But that does not make the parting any easier when it came."

Maud moved to Park Corner to stay with her Campbell relatives. "It hurts me so to think of the old house left desolate and forsaken, with no life in its rooms, no fire glowing on its hearth. Yet I am thankful that dear grandma did not suffer and that she died in her own home surrounded by beloved and familiar faces."

CHAPTER FIFTEEN

Affairs of the heart

A few weeks later, members of the Presbyterian Church in the small village of Leaskdale, seven miles or so from the Ontario town of Uxbridge, were diffidently asked by the Reverend Ewan Macdonald, their quiet Island-born minister, for a three-month leave of absence. He would be marrying Miss Lucy Maud Montgomery and he wanted a honeymoon abroad. With what has been described as true Scottish reticence, he did not enlarge on the antecedents and accomplishments of the bride-to-be; but when confronted with a copy of *Anne*, he admitted that yes, he understood she was a writer.

In July 1906, Maud had made casual mention to Mac-Millan of a friend who was about to leave for Scotland. "By the way our minister here is leaving us—Mr McDonald [*sic*]—and is going to Scotland for the winter. He will be attending college in Edinburgh I understand. I suppose it isn't in the least likely you'll ever run across him but of course it is possible. . . . We are all very sorry that he is going away as he was well-liked and a successful pastor."

They were actually engaged at the time she wrote. Ewan Macdonald, born at Bellevue in the eastern part of the Island in July 1870, came from a farm background in Valley-field, and like Maud had Scottish ancestry. Though his engagement to Maud did not take place until three years after his arrival in Cavendish in September 1903, he confessed later that he had "had his eye on her" for some time. "I understood, when I heard of the engagement," recalls an amused neighbour, "why the Reverend used to be seen sitting for long periods, and apparently aimlessly, on the bench outside the post office."

In 1906, marriage was out of the question until Grandma died, and Maud and Ewan were to be separated for much of the following five years, so that one may wonder how much opportunity the couple had for more than a fairly superficial understanding of each other's personality. Ewan spent the year 1906-07 at the United Free Church College in Glasgow, and when he returned to Canada it was not to Cavendish, but to Bloomfield and Bedeque, distant some fifty and twenty-five miles respectively. He was then called to Leaskdale, Ontario, where he was inducted on 15 March 1910.

"I remember distinctly the arrival of Maud's eventual husband, during my years in Cavendish," says Ken Macneill, seven or eight at the time. "I remember that I liked him and talked with him on numerous occasions. Naturally, at that age I would not have had any knowledge of affairs of the heart, and did not associate him with Maudie whatever. He was just a nice minister and a man who was a quarter century younger than my father, and for that very reason a little closer to me."

To MacMillan, Maud wrote her big news on page 12 of a seventeen-page letter: "I have something to tell you which may surprise you a little. Early in July I expect to be married to the Rev. Mr Macdonald whom you met in Scotland. . . . We have been engaged for five years but as I could not leave grandmother as long as she wished to remain in her old home, our engagement was kept secret."

At the end of 1906, in a November letter telling MacMillan that the "very nice and friendly" minister whose name she was still spelling McDonald had gone to Glasgow instead of Edinburgh, Maud had dispassionately offered some rather down-to-earth and unromantic ideas about love. "*Love* is a subject we haven't referred to much in our letters, but I see no reason why we should not discuss it frankly, like any other psychological problem. . . . You ask me if I believe that there is an affinity somewhere for everyone. Well, that depends on what is meant by an affinity. If you mean one who is in perfect sympathy with one's whole nature I don't think I do. I did once in the salad days of my teens but I do so no longer. I think we must take our affinities as we do our happiness—not in one long, uninterrupted stretch as I once fondly believed, but in bits here and bits there, thankful if there be no positive friction or disagreement in the natures of those we meet and mingle with. In an ideal world we might expect to meet with our ideal affinity. But in this real world, whose ragged corners rub the bloom off so many beautiful theories we can hardly expect to."

It would seem to have been impossible—at the least, unlikely—that so intensely emotional a person as Maud could escape the painful, delicious experience of falling in love. With her first sweetheart, she says, she used to sit on the school fence beneath the fir trees when she was twelve, and discuss books, particularly poems by the young man's uncle, the Reverend A. J. Lockhart, who wrote under the name of Pastor Felix (and with what rage, years later, she recorded that the firs had been cut down!). Even before that, when she was only ten, she had fallen instantly in love at a school concert with a slender, golden-haired blind young singer with the face of an angel. Though she never met or spoke to him, she treasured his memory for years.

Ewan was thirty-six at the time of the engagement, Maud thirty-two. Her son has suggested that her single status at this comparatively late age was "due partly to the fact that she had been tied down to care for her grandmother and partly to the fact that in this rural community, in those days, eligible men were few, except for somewhat earthy types." Yet she had had other reasons for remaining unmarried. In April 1907 she moved from her academic discussion with MacMillan about love and marriage into a more personal confidence. MacMillan had asked: "Do you think that love depends upon an admiration for qualities possessed by the loved one? Or is it something more subtle than this?" Maud replied: "In answer to the first question I say most emphatically 'NO'. In explaining why I think so it will be necessary for me to inflict on you a bit of my own experience. . . .

"I loved a man—let us call him A—— — once. It was emphatically the love of my life. Yet, mark this—*I did not respect him*—I did not *admire him in the least*. Before that experience I would have laughed at the idea that one *could* love a man they didn't respect. (The grammar of that sentence is shocking but never mind.) Yet I certainly did. I would not have *married* him for anything. He was my inferior in every respect. This is not vanity on my part at all. He simply was. He had no brains, no particular good looks, in short, nothing that I admire in a man. Yet I loved him as I never can love any other man. There was about him 'the subtle something' you speak of in the second part of your question. This man died and I have always been thankful that it ended so: because if he had lived I daresay I couldn't have helped marrying him and it would have been a most disastrous union in most respects."

In the light of the problems arising from her eventual choice of husband, one is tempted to wonder whether the marriage she refused ("A" was Herman Leard, a young Bedeque farmer) would have been more disastrous than the one she made. But even in the throes of what she felt had been genuine love, and clearly had been a strong physical attraction, Maud was able to subordinate her emotions to her reason. And her reason, when she was courted by Ewan Macdonald, seemed to tell her that her choice was sound. Ewan was a good-looking man with an established position in the community, and even if he had not shown outstanding mental qualities, with his Bachelor of Arts degree from Dalhousie College he was at least educated to a standard beyond that of the local farmers who were now Maud's only possible suitors.

And experience had taught her—or at least she thought it had—that a calm and rational approach to marriage, steering clear of the fatally fascinating romantic idealism and staying safely in the area of pleasant but unexciting companionship, would offer the best chance of successful marriage. She had had her high moments of ecstasy. She had also known the misery of being committed to an unsuitable engagement.

"Before I met A——," she told MacMillan, "I had met a man whom I will call B——. [This was probably her second-cousin Edwin Simpson at Belmont.] He was everything that I admire in a man—he was handsome, brilliant, cultured, successful. A—— was not worthy to tie his shoe laces. Well, I liked B—— very much. I was very young and knowing nothing of love mistook my liking and admiration for love. I became engaged to him—and then I simply hated him. Yes, laugh. I daresay you will. But it was no laughing matter to me —It was a tragedy. That man's kiss turned me cold with horror. . . . I *knew* I could *never* marry him. I tried for a year to be true to him and *hell* couldn't be worse than that year for me. In the end I told him the truth and broke the engagement. Immediately I was free I *liked* him just as well as I had before that dreadful time, but I have been haunted ever since by the wretched conviction that I have spoiled his life. He has never married and says he can't forget. . . .

"I loved one man in whom nobody could see anything to admire. I *couldn't* care for the other who was in all respects admirable. If I had married B. I should have been unhappy all my life. If I had married A. I should I believe have been *happy* but I would have deteriorated in every way. . . ."

Both Anne and Emily would live through a similar experience, Emily's engagement and near-marriage to the charming Dean Priest parallelling Maud's ill-fated affair. Maud was ready now, she thought, to settle for less—for a respected, reliable husband and a life to be lived comfortably on the plains, without the ardours and ecstasies of the high peaks.

What she looked for now, Maud wrote in September 1907, was something more practical. "After all, this is a practical world and marriage must share in its practicalities. If two people have a mutual affection for each other, don't bore each other, and are reasonably well mated in point of age and social position, I think their prospects of happiness together would be excellent, even if some of the highest up-flashings of the 'flame divine' are missing."

Her decision, in the light of the psychological problems that she was not aware of in Ewan at the time, seems to prove —if it proves anything—that reasoned thinking has no greater chance of success in marriage than romantic infatuation. "If I ever marry," continued Maud, aware as she wrote that she had already become engaged to do so, "that is the basis on which I shall found my marriage. *But*—I shall never cease to thank my fate that I *knew the other kind of love too.*"

CHAPTER SIXTEEN

Honeymoon

On Tuesday, 4 July 1911, it was announced in the Charlotte-town *Examiner* that the marriage of "the talented Island au-thoress" would take place on the following day at the home of the bride's uncle. On the same page were American reviews of *The Story Girl*, just published in book form. "It will keep a kindly smile upon your lips and in your heart as well," the Chicago *Inter-Ocean* had said. The welcoming reviews about a book Maud had truly enjoyed writing made a pleasant wed-ding gift.

The ceremony was performed by the Cavendish Presby-terian minister, the Reverend John Stirling, in the front room of Uncle John Campbell's Park Corner home, with about twenty guests present. It was followed by a great feast, prepared by Maud's cousins Stella and Frederica. For her wedding, the bride wore a dress of ivory silk crepe de chine and lace, with a tunic of chiffon and "pearl and crystal garni-ture." She carried a bouquet of white roses, lilies of the val-ley and maidenhair fern. Her veil was of tulle with a coronet of orange blossom, and she wore Ewan's gift, a pearl and amethyst necklace. As she entered the parlour at noon, unat-tended, *The Voice that breathed o'er Eden* was sung.

In the afternoon, the newlyweds left for Montreal and departure for England by the White Star liner *Megantic*. Maud's travelling dress was a suit of steel-grey serge with chiffon blouse, and a matching hat of steel-grey braid trimmed with satin rosebuds.

This trip was an especial joy, enabling Maud—as she had told the Boston reporter eight months earlier—"to verify the impressions formed by reading": and now, at last, to meet her faithful correspondent in Alloa. A flutter of short notes between June 5 and July 25, including one from the ship and a telegram, kept MacMillan informed of the travellers' plans. Maud's journal for this period was the record of a dream come true, preserving her ecstatic delight in most of the places visited, though a few failed to come up to her imaginings, and none were "more beautiful than can be seen any evening at home." With her usual preference for solitude, she revelled in the wildness of Scottish scenery on the excursion to Oban, Staffa and Iona; with her pleasure in eccentricity, she enjoyed a party of chattering French tourists until seasickness drained all interest in anything at all. But she recovered in time to make a long-dreamed-of visit to Fingal's Cave, whose grandeur silenced even the French tourists.

The Macdonalds visited the Burns country, thinking of *Tam o' Shanter* and *Highland Mary*; the Scott country, thinking of *The Lady of the Lake*—the Trossachs ("far from being the wild, riven, precipitous dell of my fancy"), Loch Lomond and Loch Katrine ("as beautiful as I had dreamed it, but . . . not my Loch Katrine"). They saw Abbotsford, Dryburgh, Melrose Abbey—not by moonlight, although "in that mellow, golden-gray evening light it was beautiful enough, with the little bluebells growing in its ruined courts and over its old graves." They stopped off in Barrie country, drove to Culloden with "a nice old driver who knew all the history and legend of everything." In mid-August they went from Edinburgh to Alloa in Clackmannanshire to visit George MacMillan.

MacMillan was now about thirty years old, and a respected *Journal* reporter. "George was really a brilliant man," one of his younger colleagues, John Gardner, has commented, "and if he'd ever summoned up the courage and initiative to leave Alloa and move to a bigger arena, he would have made a name for himself. As it was, he frequently sold small items to *Punch* and the *Strand Magazine*, and his columns and humorous poems, often in collaboration with his chief and my uncle Malcolm Gardner, the proprietor of the *Journal*, were widely enjoyed. But he suffered from a slight hypertension which may have had some bearing on his decision to remain in his home town."

MacMillan was one of four children (three sons, one daughter) of a grocer whose store was on Mill Street at the Alloa Cross. Like Maud's other correspondent, Ephraim Weber, he seems to have been largely self-educated, reared in a home not notably interested in culture, and impelled by an insatiable appetite for literature to go far beyond his ordinary borough school education. Like Maud, he had a lively curiosity about the world and its inhabitants: "conscientious in his work, unfailing in resource, and gifted with an originality which made his sketches and articles on local matters things to treasure for their easy wit and unconstrained humour. . . . He had a faculty for playful rhyming." He also wrote the words for at least one published song, and collaborated with Malcolm Gardner in several weekly features, including *Round the Bandstand, Jottings by the Way,* and *The Man in the Street.* His topical verses and parodies were apt and funny. (In later years, small Stuart, Maud's younger son, would recite some of them at concerts in Ontario's Leaskdale.) He retired in 1946, and died aged seventy-two in 1953.

MacMillan had proved, and would continue to prove to be a uniquely congenial friend for Maud. They shared so many delights, including a strong interest in astronomy: both pondered the deep mysteries of the universe with awe and fascination. "I think astronomy much the most fascinating study in the world," she wrote. She would always be enthralled by "star-hunting." A book entitled *Astronomy with the Naked Eye*, with "a chart of the constellations for every month of the year with the names of all the stars" had sent her out with a pair of good field glasses along the Cavendish roads on starry nights, and "half the time I don't know whether I'm on 'the good red earth' or roaming the Milky Way. . . . I feel as if I had literally been millions of miles away and that all my ordinary surroundings were strange and forgotten." When she read Sir James Jeans's *The Universe Around Us* in 1930, she could not agree with his theory that intelligent, conscious life must be the exception and not the rule. "It would be absurd to think God would waste so many good suns."

MacMillan was not able to offer the visitors the hospitality of his home. Instead, they were generously given accommodation by the parents of a friend and fellow-worker in various church organizations, Jean Allan. He gave the travellers a delightful tour of the beautiful neighbourhood, including Dollar Glen, "one of the wildest, grandest spots we have seen in all Scotland," Maud wrote in her journal, " . . . like a deep gash cleft down through the heart of the mountain." The *Alloa Journal* of August 12 reported her call at the office, and her verdict that "this part of the country was the finest she had yet seen."

They also visited the Glasgow Exhibition. Then, with MacMillan and Jean Allan, the honeymooners set out for a week-long tour to Spittal and the Borders, fanning out from Berwick-upon-Tweed to see the Marmion country and to explore old castles, deserted mills, Flodden Field. In a ravine at Homecliffe Glen they discovered a clump of spruce trees. The two Canadians picked the gum and ate it with familiar relish: MacMillan and Miss Allan thought it was "bitter." They all enjoyed the boat trip to Holy Island, but coming home was not so pleasant. The ladies only just avoided seasickness, and both gentlemen had to retire.

Everything about the Lake District charmed Maud. York Cathedral was "magnificent, a dream of beauty made lasting in stone." Kenilworth Castle was full of ghosts, "gay figures of olden days, living, loving, hating, plotting as of yore." Temple Church and "Poor Noll's grave" in London were outshone by a large and dignified cat, who greeted, welcomed and fare-welled them "in most irreproachable fashion."

Ewan's family tree was rooted in Skye: his father Alexander had come to Canada in 1841 at the age of seven. His mother, Christine Cameron, was Island-born, but her father had been Ewan Cameron of Skye. In Scotland, Ewan and Maud Macdonald had explored the land of their fathers, Ewan's in the Inner Hebrides, her own in Argyll: as always, listening for the ghosts of the past. Now, down the length of England and arrived in Suffolk, Maud sought eagerly for even nearer links, visiting the farm home in Dunwich where her grandmother had been a little girl. "We walked about a mile from the shore . . . until we came to the lane of the Woolner farm, now called Mount Pleasant farm. . . . Tall trees grow all through the yard and almost hide the house from sight. . . . Were these trees there in your time?" she asked her Aunt Margaret, her grandmother's sister. "It seemed as if you and grandma must be somewhere about . . . little girls of twelve and fourteen, and I thought 'if only grandma . . . were alive so that I could write about this'. . . . There is a large garden in front of the house with a hawthorn hedge around it. I picked some flowers from it and pressed them. . . . In what room of the old home were you and grandma born and where did you sleep?. . . Could you see the sea from the house then or was the view of it obscured by trees?"

Shakespeare land, Hampton Court, Stonehenge, Windsor, and London landmarks were covered in a surfeit of sightseeing. A railway strike cancelled a visit to Ireland, but the travellers carried home with them a host of memories and some solidly tangible and treasured souvenirs of their trip. How many Leaskdale old-timers still remember "John Sphinx," the little monster that sat on top of one of the bookcases in the Manse library, bringing back memories to Maud of their visit to Berwick? And there was the pair of china dogs Maud discovered in a happy moment in the shadow of York Minister, with their haunting memories of the green-spotted dogs at Grandfather Montgomery's so long ago. These were bigger, gold-spotted, and more than a hundred years old. She took them back with her when they sailed for home on the *Adriatic* at the end of September, to preside—rather incongruously in a Christian home (though Maud's impish humour would relish the incongruity)—as Gog and Magog, those leaders of the nations warring against God under Satan's direction. Her small son Chester would introduce them gravely to visitors in later years. "This one is God, and that one is *my God.*"

CHAPTER SEVENTEEN

Mistress of the Manse

Back in Leaskdale the Manse was being cleaned and painted and decorated for its new tenants. The floors were to be green: an odd instruction to people used to sober greys and browns and yellows, but this was what his lady wanted, Mr Macdonald had said. While the Reverend and his wife boarded briefly across from the church, crates were arriving: books and furniture and china were being unpacked; wedding presents, including the silver tea service presented to Maud by the Cavendish Presbyterian Church, put away.

One box, slatted on top and arriving by express, contained Daffy the Cavendish cat, now about to turn into the Leaskdale cat, so interested in him did the whole congregation become. Three days of confinement had subdued his initial vociferous protests. "He never uttered a squeak all the way from the station. . . . [Then] he climbed leisurely out and stretched himself. He was not at all hungry . . . but he was extremely thirsty and drank three saucers of milk and one of water without stopping. Then he climbed into my lap and kissed me as gravely and humanly as possible."

Most of the Leaskdale congregation hardly knew what to do with Maud, this modest, charming, friendly, unassuming, *famous* swan that had settled in their rural duckpond. They came to greet her with awe and remained to worship. Expecting to find an aloof celebrity, they found instead an unpretentious woman who chatted with them, laughed with them, cared about their joys and sorrows: seemed, in fact, like one of themselves. The congregation welcomed the Macdonalds

99

with warmth and admiration at an official church reception on a night of pouring rain. Maud piled her hair high and wore her wedding dress and charmed everyone with her graciousness.

"Leaskdale is a very pretty country place," she told MacMillan"—would be almost as pretty as Cavendish if it had the sea. . . . It is a farming settlement . . . only fifty miles from Toronto. I find the people here nice and kind. Yes, I like Leaskdale very much. But as yet I do not love it. . . . We have a nice brick manse, prettily situated, though too close to the other houses and backyards in the village to suit my love of solitude and retirement. . . . I love our library—where I hope to see you as a most welcome guest some day. The little plaque you sent . . . adorns its walls, the gilt frame harmonizing admirably with the golden brown of the wall paper."

For fifteen years at Leaskdale and nine at Norval, just west of Toronto, she performed her role in the Manse with scrupulous attention to what she felt was expected of a minister's wife, and never deviated from her script. "There are certain things that cannot be expressed in terms of dollars and cents," she wrote in *An Open Letter from a Minister's Wife* in *Chatelaine* in 1931. "The leadership which the minister's wife can give, especially in rural communities where it may otherwise be lacking, is one of them. From my viewpoint, the minister's wife has a special opportunity for service which is a privilege and not a duty." She might have been Queen Victoria (though she thought Victoria dull, and had got into trouble as a child for being candid about a portrait of that sacrosanct lady) saying "I will be good!"

In June 1912, Maud told MacMillan that she would be "entertaining the stork" next month. MacMillan's news was less happy. For a long time he seems to have cherished a hope that his friendship with Jean Allan might deepen into something more. Now he had finally faced the realization that this was not to be. Maud wrote consoling words. "I am sorry for the suffering the experience has caused you, but I believe it will all be far better for you in the end." She was still comforting him two years later for this disappointment.

Early in 1918 she heard that Miss Allan had married. But not until March 1939 did she discover, to her amazement, that Miss Allan had a brother in Toronto—the Reverend William Allan, minister at Dovercourt Road Presbyterian Church. Maud might well have been amazed. Mr Allan had been a Toronto personality for years; he had initiated the Radio Ministry in 1932 for shut-ins, and was well known for his writings and lectures. "Ever since your letter came," Maud told MacMillan excitedly, "I have been intending to get in touch with him. . . . Some of these days I will get around to seeing him." Mr Allan, unfortunately, did not have many days left. Six months later, returning to Canada from a visit to his eighty-six-year-old mother in Alloa, he was one of the victims of the *Athenia* tragedy.

Maud was nearly thirty-eight when her first son, Chester Cameron, was born in July 1912, nearly forty when Hugh Alexander was stillborn in August 1914, nearly forty-one when she had her third and last child, Ewan Stuart, in October 1915.

As to every mother, but especially to Maud with her passionate emotional intensity, this first child was a breath-taking miracle, "a dear chubby rosy little fellow. . . . I can't imagine life without him now"—her *Punch, Punch-boy, Chester-boy, Peter Pan, little Man Friday.* She noted his every development, reporting to MacMillan the moment of first real awareness in the baby eyes, the baby chatter, the first tottering steps on "small fat legs." But caring for the child, and her other duties, meant less time for writing. *The Golden Road,* published in September 1913, "was written in odds and ends of time and so left a disagreeable impression of 'unfinishedness' in my mind."

Of necessity, a life with so many compartments—mother, housekeeper, minister's wife and author—had to be organized. Without good household help, one or other would have had to be neglected. Maud was fortunate in having capable workers in the home, whose affection she earned by making them all feel welcome and valued, impressing one of them, at least, with her kindness in insisting she should eat with the family. "No, Lily. If you're good enough to be in our home, you must be at our table!"

Without being totally inflexible, housework was orderly—this day for washing, that for ironing, these for cleaning, one for baking and odd jobs, Saturdays for getting ready for Sunday. Maud enjoyed cooking, sewed well, was an expert and innovative needlewoman, designing many of her own handmade needlepoint lace patterns. Years later she was charmed to find a first prize at the Canadian National Exhibition awarded to a lace design she had originated during one long winter evening at the Cavendish farm.

She became an adept at doing two things at once: sewing while she recited or read to her children; working out plots and dialogue as she drove in the cutter or the buggy drawn by Queen, the smart little black mare; or when she travelled by train; or even as she was dressing (parishioners remember hearing "muttering" sounds from behind her closed door from time to time), crocheting or knitting during meetings and pastoral visits. She took her proper part in every aspect of church life: the pastoral visiting, the quilting parties and pie socials, the Women's Missionary Society meetings, the Young People's Guild. She was good with teen-agers, and her pleasure in reciting and reading found a welcome outlet at their gatherings and in helping them produce and act in plays. Sometimes she wrote papers on subjects that were turning over in her own mind. As early as the mid-1920s she was trying to stir up young Leaskdale minds to understand the concept of atomic energy and other deeply puzzling aspects of the universe. Maud never did anything by halves.

Through all the years in this busy round, she managed to keep a couple of hours daily for writing. "She did her writing early in the morning," says her son Stuart, "and reading late at night. As long as I can remember, she slept five hours at night—occasionally six. She was an omnivorous reader and a sight reader. She read and reread all the classic English literature, and with a fabulous memory, could quote most of Shakespeare, Wordsworth, Byron and all the famous English poets, but also read all current books, magazines and newspapers, and ate up one or two detective novels daily."

In 1912 she had published *Chronicles of Avonlea*, a book of short stories, and in 1913 *The Golden Road*, another collection of stories, dedicated to Aunt Mary Lawson. Her children's growing years, her church duties, and World War One slowed her production over the next seven years, but three of the Anne books and *The Watchman & Other Poems* (a volume of what her son has called "mediocre verse" published in Toronto in 1916 by McClelland & Stewart) appeared between 1913 and 1921.

"People around here have a nice feeling about the Macdonalds," says a Leaskdale resident. They earned the judgment. Ewan fulfilled his duties unexceptionably, preached short down-to-earth sermons, posed no intellectual threat to his congregation, was jovial and hearty. The people liked him for his dedication, his rather bluff manner. "He laughed a lot," says someone. "Pleasant, maybe a bit superficial," says another. Perhaps he used laughter to fill in awkward conversational gaps when lack of small talk was a handicap.

But Maud alone knew the depth of his personal problems. If she found him less than the stimulating companion she may have expected, it never showed in her attitude. "The Macdonalds would argue with some spirit, but never became angry with each other," recalls a woman who worked in their home.

Nor did the congregation ever realize, as Maud soon did, how deeply Ewan could sink into a state of nervous melancholia. She wrote casually to friends about his ill health—his "nervous prostration," his insomnia, his low spirits. But only at the very end of her life did she disclose the despair for her husband's state of mind that had filled her heart for most of their life together: and by then, other burdens had combined to bow her down.

CHAPTER EIGHTEEN

Terrors
and triumphs

The war was a dreadful drain on Maud's mental and physical health, aggravated at the very beginning by the stillborn birth of her second child. Her letters to MacMillan during these years make painful reading, full of terrors and turmoil and agony of spirit. "Oh, is it not hideous—unbelievable—unthinkable! . . . Oh, surely, surely, Germany cannot win! . . . It is no joke but a simple fact that I have not had one decent dinner since the war began. Our *dinner* hour is one. The mail comes in at 12.30. If the news is good it excites me, if it is bad it upsets me and I can eat little. While if I decide to exert all my will-power and refuse to look at the papers until after dinner the suspense is worst of all and I can eat absolutely nothing. When I tell this to our comfortable, stolid country people who, from a combination of ignorance and lack of imagination, do not seem to realize the war at all, they laugh as if they thought I was trying to be funny. Those who perceive that I am in earnest think I am crazy."

She was passionately sure it was a righteous war for which she favoured conscription and to which she would send her own sons were they old enough. She argued vehemently with Weber's view that it was a commercial war. "When Germany outraged Belgium and swooped down on France," she shot back, "would you have had England sit still without lifting a finger?" She could not believe that the world would ever outlaw war. "There may be universes—worlds—where this is not the case; but ours is not one." Why argue about it, she told Weber, the idealist; neither would convince the other.

By January 1916, the demands of three-month-old Stuart—
"our wee blue-eyed laddie"—were added to work with the
Red Cross. Maud filled "every available chink and cranny
of time" with sewing and knitting for the Red Cross (she was
president of the local branch) and helping pack huge bales
of supplies. By this time, reality had brought home to Leaskdale what Maud's sensitivity had made her suffer from the
beginning. To Weber, she wrote: "In Uxbridge, our little
market town seven miles away a regiment is billeted for the
winter, and about seventeen of our finest boys have enlisted
right here in our little rural community. Our church on
Sunday is full of khaki uniforms, and oh, the faces of the
poor mothers! The church is full of stifled sobs as my husband
prays for the boys at the front and in training." Many of her
own cousins and friends were in the trenches "somewhere in
France," including her half-brother, twenty-two-year-old Carl.
The following year, Carl would lose a leg, blown off at Vimy
Ridge, where he lay on the snow-covered battlefield eighteen
hours before being rescued. Yet, back in Toronto, he was
"brown and hearty, cheerful and jolly, and gets around quite
smartly on his one leg. A cripple in his young manhood!"

In October 1915, Stuart's birth had been followed by
Ewan's six-week bout of bronchitis and a series of illnesses
for Maud that ended in anaemia and loss of energy. The war
news was all bad. "I shall never forget the agony of those two
weeks when it seemed likely that the Germans were going to
smash their way through! It was just when everything here
was at its worst—E's illness and my own break-down. I
couldn't eat or sleep. I *grew old* in that fortnight."

For someone whose very nearest and dearest were not involved in the war, and who was far from any scene of danger,
her agonizing might be thought self-indulgent, not easy to
understand except in the light of her volatile emotional
response to every kind of experience. Her intensity transformed and magnified everything that happened to her. It
was not hard for Maud's sensitive heart to suffer the pangs of
the truly bereaved and the horrors of the battlefield.

She began to examine her dreams for omens and premonitions, drawing what favourable interpretations she could

from their various elements: the frightful storm, for instance, from which a khaki-clad soldier had rushed into the Manse for refuge, and the sudden clearing of the skies, when she found herself crowned with flowers. "You may smile," she told MacMillan. "But in the terrible weeks of the Verdun offensive that dream was really my only comfort. . . . But one night during the height of the second desperate effort of the Germans, even my dream failed to sustain me. I seemed to go all to pieces. I walked the floor in nervous agony, picturing the worst . . . but towards morning I fell into a sound sleep. . . . When I awoke I was perfectly calm . . . I felt serene and confident. . . . Whether my subconscious mind really has in some way . . . foreseen the predestimed end of the struggle, time only can show."

Another "storm" dream seemed to forecast the attack on Rumania. "I dreamed that I was in the old sitting room down home with some friends. Suddenly we noticed a gloom and, running to the window I saw that exactly half the sky from the horizon to the zenith was covered with a dense black pall which seemed to have risen up in a moment. As I looked one livid, jagged bolt of lightning rent it asunder. We all ran to do various things as a preparation for the storm—shutting doors, closing shutters, driving in chickens etc. Then when everything was done we discovered that there was no longer *any* storm to prepare for—the sky was clear, the sun shining. I woke at once with the conviction that another German offensive was coming but from what quarter I could not imagine. When the attack on Roumania began I never doubted that Bucharest would fall—I believed that was what the bolt of lightning foretokened. Assuredly the first half of my dream came true," wrote Maud, convinced her interpretation was valid. "The war! Oh, the war!" During the long-drawn-out Verdun offensive, she had felt "as if I were slowly bleeding to death."

Her ninth strange dream since the outbreak of war ("and *every one* has come true") occurred in March 1918, when she held a newspaper whose headline proclaimed "There are 30 evil days in store for us." Next night she dreamed again; she was standing on a great plain "and I held in my arms a man whose face I could not see but whom I knew to be dying. As I held him he died and fell from my arms to the ground. Then I saw his face—and it was the face of the Kaiser's *father*. . . ." For Maud, this foretold the defeat of the House of Hohenzollern.

At every crisis she had spent sleepless nights. Until she heard that Jutland had been a victory and not a defeat, "I walked the floor like a lunatic." The shelling of Paris gave her a night that seemed "an endless agony." On the death of Kitchener, who with Lloyd George was one of her heroes, she felt that "one of the props of the Empire had been wrenched away." At meetings during the conscription election, she spoke twice on Women's Responsibility. In June 1918 she dreamt she met Marshal Foch "and he said simply, 'October 3rd.' " When the war was over, she convinced herself that the dream had been predictive. "You may remember," she told MacMillan, "that on October *4* Prince Maximilian announced before the German Reichstag that it had been decided to ask for an armistice. That announcement was made on the *fourth*. Does it not seem reasonable to suppose that the *decision* to ask for an armistice was made on the *third?*"

Despite the tremendous tensions, the daily routine of home and church and authorship had to go on. In January 1917, Stuart, who "is said to look like me," was walking and talking. Five-year-old Chester, a "chip off the old block," was "about as comfortable to have around as a young elephant": annoyed at his mother for some unappreciated restraint, he had just marched out of the room (Maud wrote to MacMillan) announcing, "If you act like that *at* me, mother, I'll turn you into a pig."

Over the years, MacMillan had been pondering the idea of writing a book, perhaps of essays, or in the form of letters. Maud encouraged him with ideas for topics and titles. The book was never written, but MacMillan's humorous verse earned him a local reputation. Maud liked his "Sweet" song in the *Alloa Journal* in October 1917, a rueful comment on the imminent sugar rationing.

Out-of-town trips for business, for duty and for pleasure, made inroads on her time. Maud was now in constant demand for speaking engagements or to give readings from her own work. She dashed off to Montreal; to Warsaw, Indiana, to visit Ewan's brother; to Boston where an unfortunate lawsuit had been shaping up over a disagreement with her original publisher, the L. C. Page Company. Page had included the right of refusal of all books she might write for five years after the signing of her contract with them in 1907, and she now found other reasons for wishing to be free from their restrictions. They had "kept me in misery for a year," Maud wrote in November 1917.

In 1917, too, she felt she had been too long away from the Island: perhaps a two-year absence had dried up her inspiration. She was writing articles for Canadian publications—this was the year that the story of her career, *The Alpine Path*, appeared in the Toronto magazine *Everywoman's World*. She sent a copy to MacMillan, and little poems by Canadian writers who might never have made the overseas scene dotted the pages of the *Alloa Journal*. But as for serious work, she had no time to produce more than pot-boilers, she said; only when leisure returned did she feel she could try to write something nearer "literature." In 1919 she was writing exultantly of six weeks in Prince Edward Island during the summer of the previous year. And this time she ventured to enter her old home: on an earlier visit, she had dared do no more than gaze at it from outside.

"It was a sad sight. The old maple grove was gone and most of the old birches. How sorrowful, how forlorn the old house looked.

"I slipped around to the back and saw that the door was secured only by a wire easily unfastened. I did what I never expected to do again—I opened the door and once more crossed the old threshold. I stood in the old kitchen. It was quite clearly visible in the dusk. A damp odor of decaying plaster hung heavy on the air. I went through the sitting room and the parlor. In each I shut my eyes and *thought myself* back into the past. Everything was around me as of old—each picture, each chair, each book or flower in its old place. I went up the dark stairs. I stood on the threshold of my old room—my old small illimitable kingdom where I had written my books long ago. But I did not go in. The window was boarded up and the room was as dark as midnight. Somehow I could not enter it. It was too full of ghosts—lonely, hungry ghosts. They would have pulled me in among them and kept me. I would have disappeared forever from the land of living men and nobody would ever have known what had become of me!

"Then I went down and out and away. These pilgrimages to shadow land are eerie things with an uncanny sweetness. I think I will make no more of them."

The Island had never been so lovely, so scented, so alluring, still the hiding-place of fairies secreted in wild columbine bells. As long as she lived, Maud Montgomery would need the Island to refresh her spirit. But such happiness made her apprehensive. "The gods do not give such gifts out of mere wantonness of giving. They are meant as consolation prizes for dark days to follow." Her old haunts still knew her for their own; but she left the Island with the chilling conviction that never again would it be so delightful.

Illness followed on the heels of exultation: a winter of influenza and neurasthenia, another visit to Boston for the lawsuit she had brought against Page. A fatal hole in her original 1907 contract lost Maud thousands of dollars when the movie rights for *Anne of Green Gables* were sold. Who in 1907 would have thought of protecting possible movie and dramatic rights? —and, at that, for a book intended for the shelves of Sunday School libraries? It seems vastly unfair that the creator of the character without whom there would have been no movie should have been denied any part of the profits. But the law came down against Maud this time. She never received one cent from either of the two movies made from the book, nor from the plays that were written from it.

Her grievances against the Page Company were not over. "Next year they're likely to publish a 'new' book by me," she warned Weber, "but be not deceived. It is a collection of old short stories which they held for years under the old contract but would never publish so long as they could get anything better."

Some of the stories had been published before. *The Son of His Mother* had appeared in *The Canadian Magazine* in March 1904; *The Hurrying of Ludovic*, its community of Deland River now transformed into Avonlea and its young plotter Juliet into Anne, had appeared in the same publication in May 1905, and Maud had brought the story of Ludovic and his lady-love Theodora Dix into Avonlea when *Anne of the Island* was published in 1915. *Everybody's Magazine* had used *The Quarantine at Alexander Abraham's* in April 1907. The book was duly published in 1920 as *Further Chronicles of Avonlea.* "Don't read it," Maud advised Weber.

CHAPTER NINETEEN

Lawsuit

This publication initiated nine years of lawsuits in which neither stubborn Maud nor stubborn Page would retreat. In ten pages of a February 1929 letter to MacMillan, when it was finally all over, she recounted the sorry tale.

"And now I am going to expound a dark secret which I promised should be revealed to you in the fulness of time. You remember your surprise when you found on Harrap's list of my books a certain one 'Further Chronicles of Avonlea' which you never knew existed. Well, 'thereby hangs a tale'— a tale that would fill a volume but must be condensed into a few pages. For the past *nine years* my existence has been to a certain extent a nightmare because of 'Further Chronicles.'

"As you know L. C. Page Co. of Boston were my first publishers. . . . When they accepted *Anne of Green Gables* (because a P.E.I. girl on their staff gave them no peace till they did) they asked me if I would prefer a royalty or a certain sum outright. I know now they thought I would jump at 'the certain sum' in which case I would have got $500 for *Green Gables*. But green as I was I was not so green as that so I said 'a royalty.' The contract was a hard one even for a beginner and one clause in it was that I must give them all my books on *the same lines* for a period of five years. I did not think this mattered because I never dreamed Green Gables was going to be a big success so I willingly signed up.

"In 1912 I had no new book ready so the Pages asked me to send them all my short stories for a volume to fill in. I sent them all I had of any value at all. They selected the best and 'Chronicles of Avonlea' were published. They sent back the rest but *unknown to me kept copies of them.* I destroyed the MSS they returned as I did not think they would ever be needed again. I may say that I had rewritten all the stories largely and added a good deal of new material mostly description. These new descriptive bits I kept and used them from time to time in various books that followed—The Golden Road, Anne of the Island etc. etc. This is an important point —keep it in memory.

"By 1916 I found it impossible to carry on with the Page Co. any longer. All their authors had left them and I was compelled to do so too. The time limit had now expired so I went to Stokes. Page was furious and threatened lawsuits to no end but in the end he did nothing because he hadn't the shadow of a claim anywhere.

"The next year he kept back $1000 out of my royalties on the ground that I had been overpaid previously. I needn't go into these details. Page's record is full of these things when dealing with his women writers. He . . . knew most women would submit to anything rather than go to law. But I came of a different breed of cats. I got the Authors League of America to find me a good Boston lawyer, and I entered suit in 1919 and *won it.* The judge gave me the $1000 dollars.

"Page had now found out there was no chance of bull-dozing me and his lawyer . . . (a very fine man by the way) approached me with an offer to buy my rights in the books entirely out. I was as anxious to get rid of them as they were to be rid of me, so I named a sum which would bring me in as much income every year if permanently invested as the royalties on the books were. After long dickering they came up to my price but on one condition. They asked me to allow them to publish another volume of short stories—those stories they had returned in 1912. This is where I made my mistake. I should never have done it. But I was terribly worried at the time, having just got word of the fatal illness of my dear friend Frede Campbell [her cousin Mrs. MacFarlane] in Montreal and I wanted to get away at once and be free, as I fondly fancied of the Page Co. for ever more. Besides they insinuated a vague threat that they could get those stories from the original magazines and publish them any time they

112

liked—the very year I was bringing out a new book perhaps. So, as the stories were poor stuff, I agreed. I was to send copies of the stories. Of course being bound to Stokes I had to get their consent which they freely gave on *condition that there would be no mention of Anne* in the book. So the contract was drawn up and the Pages given the right to publish the book in 1920. I went home, sent them copies of the stories and thought no more about them.

"Then in the fall of 1919 Page wrote me that they had 'discovered in their vaults copies of the stories I had sent in 1912 and were going to publish *them* as the contract gave them the right to do.' I was aghast. Not only were there pages of description in those old MS that by this time had been used in succeeding books but there were several appearances of *Anne* in them—inserted when I was preparing them for possible inclusion in the first 'Chronicles'. This meant a breach of my contract with Stokes and would lay me open to breach of contract suit from them if they wanted to be nasty. Also I would be made absurd by a book coming out under my name containing no end of paragraphs and descriptions which were to be found in my other books.

"I got my lawyer to notify Page that they had no right to publish the 1912 versions and I would bring suit against them if they did. But they did it and brought out 'Further Chronicles' in March 1920. I at once brought suit for an injunction against the book and damages to my literary reputations. The case came up in May 1920. I went down to Boston for it. Page's lawyer thought the case would be over in *two days*. My lawyer was not so optimistic and thought it would take three. *It took nearly nine years!*

"Page's regular lawyer would not take the case so they got [another one]. . . . By the time two days were over it became evident that it was going to be longer than they thought so it went before a 'Master'. This Master hears the evidence at leisure, gives his opinion thereon and hands it to the judge who decides accordingly.

"*I had to stay in Boston until the middle of July.* I was on the witness stand for *three weeks* on end, being cross-examined by the ablest lawyer at the Boston bar. Can you fancy a more nerve-wracking ordeal. But I was telling the truth and not afraid to tell it and he could not break me down. You have heard no doubt of 'the maddening delays of the law'. Well, I know all about them. The hardest thing was their lawyer's 'trick' questions. But, 'though I say it as hadn't orter' he never trapped me once. And when it came to *my* lawyer's turn to grill the Page brothers *we* got some fun out of it—for they . . . would get all tangled up and contradict themselves and each other.

"Of course the whole thing hinged on the interpretation of the contract and their lawyer dragged in something every day to befog the issue. One day my lawyer got George Page to admit a certain thing and after the session he said to me 'We've won our case. I was afraid we couldn't get him to admit that.'

"But we were a long way from winning it. The lawyers would spend *hours* wrangling over the admissibility of certain questions or evidence and for days we would make no progress at all that I could see. Just think of my worry. And one of my boys ill at home! And yet that battle of wits between trained intellects was amazingly fascinating and if I had not been the toad under the harrow I would have enjoyed it.

"*One whole day* those three grave lawyers and myself wrangled over the exact color of *Anne's* hair and the definition of 'Titian' red. Ye gods, it *was* funny. The big table was snowed under with literature and prints to disprove or prove. They had two 'art experts' on the stand who flatly contradicted each other. Years before when I sat down in that old house in Cavendish one rainy spring evening and dowered Anne with red tresses I did not dream that a day would come when it would be fought over in a Boston courtroom. Their lawyer was determined to prove that Titian hair was dark red and that I knew it was dark red. I didn't. I always supposed it was a sort of flame-red and I stuck to it through all his badgerings. One expert said it was 'bright golden-auburn' and the other said it was the color of burnished copper. And so on!

"The raison d'etre of all this was the picture of the red-headed girl on the cover which was a part of our case.

"By the end of June the Pages evidently thought that the

case was not going to be over as soon as they had hoped and decided to hurry it up a bit by scaring me into dropping it. They handed me a writ, suing me for $30,000 damages for libel because of the statements in my 'bill of complaint.' This was absurd of course. A bill of complaint is privileged and they had no case. But the trouble is in the States you have to pay your own fees and costs whether you win or lose and the wealthy Page Co. could afford that better than I could. But my fighting blood was up and I determined to ignore their threat and fight to the end. Still, you can imagine the worry and vexation this inflicted on me.

"Then a Page witness swore to a flat lie—a most damaging lie to our case and my lawyer lost his grit. He said it was such damaging testimony that he thought we'd better offer to settle. I would *not* knuckle down to the Pages after the way they had behaved and said so. So on we went.

"I came home in mid-July a perfect wreck. But the case went on.

"In September Page's lawyer filed his damage suit for the libel. Then the Master took *nearly a year* to make up his report. In September 1921 it came—and it was decidedly adverse to us. I had never expected anything else, of course, after the lies. . . . The report was sent to the judge but it is a *very* rare thing that a judge does not follow the Master's findings. As for the libel suit in August 21 it was thrown [out] of the Massachusetts court on the ground that it was illegal. Then Page appealed it to the Supreme Court of the State. In six months it was thrown out there. Then he carried it to the Supreme Court of the United States!

"As for the Master's report, handed in in Sept. 1921 would you believe it was *April 1923* before the judge gave his decision. Such a thing was never heard of I believe. But—perhaps it was as well for me because what happened was that the judge discarded the Master's report and examined all the evidence himself. There was about a trunkful of typewritten evidence and he told my lawyer he had never met such an interesting case in his life. *And he gave decision in my favour!* I got my injunction against the book and *all* the profits.

"Oddly enough the very same day word came that the Page

appeal had been thrown out by the Supreme Court of the U.S.

"Do you think my worry was over then? Not by a jugful! Of course the Pages at once appealed from the judge's decision.

"And in December 1923 they filed the same old libel suit in the courts of *New York State* and attached my royalties due from Stokes to compel me to fight the case over again there. A New York lawyer had to be engaged also!

"In June 1924 the New York suit was dismissed. Then Page appealed to the Supreme Court of New York.

"On March 4, 1925, the appeal in my case was decided in my favour.

"Then they had to begin the 'accounting' to find out what the 'profits' really were. In October 1925 the New York libel case was finally thrown out and my long withheld royalties paid to me. My N.Y. lawyer wrote me that, since I was not a resident of N.Y. State I had a clear case against the Page Co. for the repayment of all the N.Y. suit had cost me. It had cost me $2000. So I thought I would show Page I had plenty of fight left in me yet and I at once entered suit in New York against *him*!

"In June 1927 the judge gave decision on the profits in my favor. The Pages appealed the amount. In March 1928 I won my New York suit and got back my money.

"And *finally* in October 1928 the Page appeal was refused. *At last* there was nothing more they could do by hook or crook. They paid me $18,000 of profits and the thing was ended after nearly 9 years of worry and expense. The suit cost me $15,000. So I had for recompense $3000, my injunction against the book—*and* the satisfaction of having whipped the Pages to a finish!

"The suit cost the Pages about $75,000 in all. And for the past four years they and their lawyer have not been on speaking terms, though he continued to act for them.

"Those are just the *outlines*! The details would fill a library! . . .

"I began this letter Feb. 10. It is now March 10—and spring—and housecleaning. But, thank God, *no lawsuits*!"

CHAPTER TWENTY

Minister's wife

Perhaps she should never have married a minister. There was more than a grain of seriousness in her rueful comment to MacMillan in 1927 that "Those whom the gods wish to destroy they make ministers' wives!" Certainly she should never have married Ewan Macdonald, whose intense and tragic personal problem—a belief that he was predestined to hell—made itself apparent only slowly to Maud in his increasingly distressing melancholia. Even beneath the shelter of an untroubled marriage, Maud would probably have found difficulty in maintaining the checks and limits on her patience. But once committed, she was not the person to withdraw from the loyalty demanded of a wife—and of a minister's wife at that.

It was not an easy life for a positive person with emphatic views often at variance with what had to be her outward behaviour in a small and conventional community; and now the heavy demands of church work on her time were added to those of her role as a popular author. Her own moral standards, her own willingly shared emotional riches within the bounds of propriety, these brought her well-deserved respect. But for Maud Macdonald too many questions did not find answers, or found answers that could have earned her the scandalized rejection of her congregation had she openly expressed them, though many of them were little more than a sturdy refusal to accept narrowmindedness and meanness of spirit.

It was the legacy—and perhaps the curse—of her upbringing, in which the strength of her own powers of reason and a natural and spontaneous warmth of heart were subordinated to the forbidding Calvinism of Presbyterian dogma. Maud had been an amenable, eager-to-please child, trying to accept the edicts of her elders as right and proper. The adult Maud had learned to question and rebel. But the loyalty to her husband that made her a genuine helpmeet; loyalty to the role she had accepted in society; loyalty to her status as a writer read by the young: all these demanded that no public expression of her inner self, where it deviated from accepted beliefs, should ever be allowed. A tug-of-war conscience did not make for easy balance between training and inclination; she found she was "compelled to play the part by the circumstances of my existence." That no hint of this unceasing internal battle reached those among whom she moved is a tribute to the strength of her personality.

Her congregation would have been astonished by the questing spirit and emphatically unorthodox opinions simmering behind that quiet, friendly face, and they never realized the iron control that kept her at her post, nor understood the pull of weariness and her need for solitude and escape.

She catalogued to Weber and MacMillan the tiresome details of a typical week. Tonight, rehearsal for a play being got up by the Guild. Last night, out to tea. Sunday night to song service. Saturday night a function at Zephyr (the other church in the Leaskdale charge), where she gave an address and presented a gift to a departing member of the Women's Missionary Society. Friday night conducting a Guild social. Thursday night, "practice" again for the play. Wednesday, a trip to Toronto to hear Lloyd George speak. Tuesday night, pastoral visiting. Monday night, practice again.

In 1920, as "a sort of duty" she sat up late at a young farmer's wedding reception. "I had to sit there till two in the morning and talk to scores of the women who were sitting in rows around the room, until I felt like a machine that just talked ever on without any volition. My head ached, my back ached, my mind and soul ached," listening to chatter about hens, eggs, new babies, the high cost of living, "and all the other entrancing subjects of 'conversation' which prevail hereabouts—at least when 'the minister's wife' is present." She suspected that when she was absent the people would talk "racy and malicious and *interesting* gossip, and enjoy themselves much better, but alas, ministers' wives dare not meddle with gossip, else would their tenure in the land be short and troubled."

When she had been a young teacher at Bideford on the Island, she had sent to a Toronto magazine a sample of her handwriting for character analysis. "You are of a rather domineering disposition," she was told, "but knowing how to master yourself as well as others, are very controlled. You are very fond of elegance and luxury, of aristocratic manners, etc. *You know how to suppress and hide your internal thoughts and feelings to such an extent as to appear utterly different from what you really are.* You can be extremely amiable, affable and obliging. You have a will of your own. You like comfort and ease. You are very economical, very politic and diplomatic, suspicious and distrustful. I could tell you a great many more things from your very interesting handwriting."

The italics were Maud's own. While she wondered what "the other things" were that might have been revealed, she commented to MacMillan, "I consider that the underlined sentence marked me out and predestined me for a minister's wife!!!" And though character analysis from handwriting is far from an exact science, this summary was not far from the truth about Maud.

She kept herself beyond criticism, knowing full well the avalanche of censure that would destroy her if she should wander from the accepted paths of behaviour. Those among whom she moved with such cheerful warmth could never have known the tightness of the rein by which she held herself in check, nor the violence with which she repudiated her reputation for social grace, as if she felt it was a mask she was forced to wear. She was not a mixer, though she knew she was considered to be a good one. "I hate the word." She was only "an excellent imitator of one." She *detested* mixers, and despised herself for having to ape them. "I never knew a 'good mixer' yet that was worth a brass farden." The only really worthwhile people were "cats who walked by themselves, rejoicing in their own peculiar brand of cathood and never pretending to be Maltese if they were tortoise shell. . . . You know as well as I do," she told Weber, "that the mixer has no real influence at all"—like a *catalyzer* ("or is it catalyst?") in chemistry, helping but not influencing.

To the young salesman who offered the range of volume as a selling point for irreverent Sunday listening to the Victrola, Maud was sternly the minister's wife. What, she demanded, would her congregation think if they heard her playing *dance* music, even softly, while Ewan was away preaching? Some of them would have understood; many more would have been disillusioned, and she could not risk that— not only for Ewan's sake, but for her own belief in what was a proper example. So she held herself in check. She who had loved dancing denied herself the indulgence as unbecoming to her new role. And "what agonies I have endured betimes when I was dying to laugh" (or criticize, or speak sharply, or contradict, or withdraw?) "but dared not because I was the minister's wife."

What would many of her people have thought, too, of some of her shockingly unorthodox thoughts? Reading W. E. H. Lecky's controversial *History of European Morals from Augustus to Charlemagne*, she agreed with his views on suicide. "Life is forced upon us; we did not ask for it; therefore if it becomes too hard we have a right to lay it down," though such an act would be cowardly if it laid a burden on others. She took issue with Lecky's belief that conscience was divinely implanted. "Conscience is merely the result of our education in right and wrong, and is not in itself an infallible guide. Bitter experience usually teaches us results of words and deeds . . . and so far guides us, but Christians have burned each other quite persuaded that the Apostles would have done the same."

For many years she had been drawn to a belief in reincarnation, the afterglow, probably, of her passion for Zanoni. As early as 1906 she had written: "It is fascinating to suppose that we go from one existence to another, with the restful sleep of so-called death between! To me, the idea is a thousand fold [more] attractive than that of the Christian's heaven with its unending *spiritual* joys." And more than thirty years later she still hopefully clung to the same possibility. In 1937 she confided to Ephraim Weber that she believed the soul to be immortal, but not personalities. When the body was worn out, "the undying spark within us joins the flood of life pervading the universe, seeks and finds another 'robe of flesh' and proceeds to build up another personality. *No* other belief, it seems to me, can explain or justify the problems and pains of life. If this present life is but a *day* in a year of days—they shrink to unimportance . . . in the course of eternity we will live *all* kinds of lives and undergo *all* kinds of experiences, thereby attaining to perfect wisdom and understanding."

But she gave little credence to spiritualism, shattering its claims with shafts of humour. The sudden death in mid-1919 of her cousin Frederica Campbell MacFarlane had given Maud "the most terrible blow I ever had to bear in all my life." They had made a pact years before that the first to die would communicate with the other if possible, but *none returneth again that is gone thither*, and there was no message. "I only know that I am left desolate, bereft . . . whither has she gone? Across the gulf of separation there comes no response. . . . She took away with her the laughter of life for me."

When Maud read *The Twentieth Plane* by Dr Albert Durrant Watson, edited by Dr Albert Holden Abbott, instructor in philosophy and assistant in the psychological laboratory in the University of Toronto, then president of the Canadian Society for Psychic Research, she found it pathetically funny because "so oddly serious." The spiritualists "are choice in the spook company they keep," she commented. "There isn't a single non-famous spirit on their calling list, except Dr. Watson's mother. Shakespeare and Plato, Wordsworth and Lincoln etc. etc. jostle each other for a chance to expound through the ouija board—and all use precisely the same literary style, and a very awful one at that. There don't seem to be any grocers or butchers or

121

carpenters on the Twentieth Plane. . ." And she would prefer more substantial fare than synthetic beef tea and the juice of a rice product, "if one must eat in the world of spirits," and a pleasanter environment in which to consume the food than in a pink twilight under an orange sun.

She came from the tragedy of her loss to the ouija-board craze endorsed by author and editor of the book, and found it unconvincing—"and I was so ready to be convinced." Ouija was remarkably flippant with Maud. When the company stopped asking it questions, it piped up of its own accord.

"Now Laura will dance! Tee hee!"

"But, Ouija, I have no music, I can't dance without music!"

"Oh, Maud will whistle."

For some reason Ouija always spelled phonetically when Maud was at the board ("Why? I detest the idea."). And when asked to name her worst fault, Ouija gave Maud the cryptic reply, *Ewan knows.*" That the board might be right, she admitted. "But evidently some demons have a sense of humor."

In 1924 she was hailing science as the source of the new revelation she felt sure must be coming. "The older revelations have exhausted their mandate. I believe the next one will come through science. What form it will take I cannot guess. . . . Two thousand years ago Jesus Christ burst the bonds that were stifling human thought. Now these bonds are tightening around us again—outworn dogmas, dead superstitions. It will take something as tremendous in its own way as his message for spiritual freedom to destroy those bonds again. But—it will come."

Five years later she was still thinking along the same lines. "Humanity has to pay some price for growing up and becoming wise and rich and comfortable . . . we are, I believe, entering on an age of wonderful scientific development. We will do things that are hardly dreamed of as yet but we will not write great literature or paint great pictures. We can't have everything at the same time. We will fly round the world—and solve the secret of the atom, but there will be no Shakespeares or Homers. They went out with the gods."

As early as 1927 she had been apprehensive about the atomic future. "It will be wonderful and revelatory—but will it be beautiful? The discovery of a way to release the energy of the atom will be the next epochal thing after the dynamic of Jesus. I hope it will not come in my time, nor in my children's. Because it will mean the overturning and passing away of all existing conditions, whether of good or evil. Everything will go—our financial institutions, our standards of value, our ways of living. An utterly new world will arise —which may be a very good thing for those who will be accustomed to it, and who will look back to our age as one lost in darkness and ignorance." But there would be some things still hidden. "God will always keep a few secrets to himself," she added nearly two years later when she was feeling "both infinitesimal and infinite. And a little dizzy," after reading Charles Henshaw Ward's *Exploring the Universe*.

She retained her old abhorrence of "the traditional paths of thought and expression" in teaching Christian ideals. "To this day," she wrote in 1922, her picture of a Christian was not that of someone trying to carry out the ideals and ideas of Jesus, but of an individual like the unctuous evangelist at Cavendish. In time, "I was able to separate this attitude and came into my heritage of reverence for that unique and wonderful personality with its lofty aspirations, its pure conception of truth, its radical scorn for outworn conventions and dogmas." But she found it painful to see her own children in their turn subjected to "false and ugly conceptions of these matters," and to be unable to interfere because her husband's position demanded discretion.

But once, at least, she resolved "to dare the Leaskdale Grundyites." Seven-year-old Stuart, learning his catechism, came to the question *Why did God make all things?* Answer: *For His own glory.* "It seemed to me an abominable libel on God," she wrote in outrage. With scorn for his teachers, "a couple of crude, ignorant old women who never had an original thought in their lives," who regarded as the deepest dyed infidel anyone who did not believe in "the talking snake of Eden," she told Stuart: "That is not how that question should be answered. God made all things for the love and pleasure of creating them—of doing good work—of bringing beauty into existence."

Though she might rage inwardly and despise adherence to the letter where it damaged the spirit, those who knew and loved her in Leaskdale and Norval were not mistaken in their judgment of her. For all her unorthodoxy, Maud Montgomery Macdonald remained an intensely spiritual woman, with a loving heart and an inviolable sense of duty. Everything she wrote rings with a deep inner truth, a hope that decency, morality, beauty will prevail, a revulsion from the limited vision of pettiness, though she knew her own frailties, and sometimes could not cleanse her own soul of pettiness. She had the wisdom to recognize, at least, the unimportance of what she rejected, the importance of what she still believed. Her congregations might have been shocked by some of her views, but the life she lived among them must surely have spoken in a louder voice.

*The Manse at Leaskdale, Ontario, Maud's first married home.
Here her sons were born.*

St. Paul's Church, Leaskdale, Ontario

The Manse at Norval, Ewan Macdonald's second Ontario charge

The Presbyterian Church, Norval, Ontario

Maud,
front and centre,
with one of
her amateur
theatrical companies

L.M. Montgomery

*Stuart (three) and Chester
(six) with their father in
the garden at Leaskdale*

*Maud's younger son,
Stuart, aged about four*

*Chester Macdonald, Maud's
elder son, aged three*

*Stuart Macdonald became
national junior gymnastic
champion in 1933.*

"I love best the flowers I coax into bloom myself."
A happy Maud Macdonald in the 1930s

*The Reverend and Mrs. Ewan Macdonald with Stuart (left)
and Chester, at Leaskdale*

*Maud's cousin Beatrice McIntyre went with the family on an
unforgettable trip in 1924 to the Mammoth Cave in Kentucky.*

Springtime at Norval. Gardening was one of Maud's greatest delights.

L.M. Montgomery in 1935

Maud's "love of pussies" shows up in the little cat-symbol she often used with her signature.

CHAPTER TWENTY-ONE

Demands
of duty

Maud could easily have allowed herself to be remembered differently in Leaskdale. Famous authors can be aloof, superior, condescending—and so, of course, can ministers' wives. But Maud Macdonald—minister's wife and world-famous author—is remembered with love by the people of her congregation: with more than love—a glow of admiration, and a little astonishment that she had seemed like one of themselves.

It was hardly possible for Maud to be unaware of her effect on her congregation, nor to fail to enjoy it, a perfectly human reaction. As a child, she had revelled in being at centre-stage, even if the position had been gained painfully, as when she had so severely burned her hand. She would have had to be aware that she stood on some kind of pedestal—nor, in fact, was it possible for the congregation to look at her with any kind of objectivity. They observed with fascinated attention everything she did, this woman who talked to them and laughed with them and sorrowed with them and moved among them as an equal; with them, but hardly of them.

There was no cold calculation in her own image of herself, nor was it a false image. Duty demanded that she be publicly true to her role, and, as always, duty was her guide. It was a duty that she regarded as a privilege; but it was also a wearying role for one who secretly abhorred "mixers," the more wearying because she accepted also the tiresome responsibilities of successful authorship. It is vastly to her credit that she juggled a tight domestic routine, a voluminous correspondence, the demands of public appearances and a warm community fellowship with its thousand calls on her time and sympathy, along with her private disappointments and secret rebellions—all without a single crack in the facade of her reputation.

How many times did she subordinate her own desires and preferences to the demands of common courtesy, of duty? A perceptive Leaskdale friend remembers travelling with her by train to a nearby town and being gently requested to forgive her apparent remoteness: she liked to use the time for thinking out some tricky scene in her current work. "Yet, when acquaintances chanced to board the train at an intermediate stop and join us with incessant, inconsequential chatter, no one would ever have guessed, from Mrs. Macdonald's demeanor, how unwelcome their intrusion must have been."

The people of Leaskdale have treasured with deep affection the happy trivia of life in the Manse. The bone-handled pen with which Maud wrote at a table strewn with ink bottle, notebooks, papers and Daffy the cat; her uninhibited enjoyment in what she wrote, rippling over her face in smiles and sometimes breaking into laughter; the little velvet bows she liked to wear on her blouses; her beautiful rose satin dress with lace-overlaid bodice; the sturdy fur-lined coat of blue broadcloth in which she braved winter driving, wrapped around with additional coats and scarves; the graceful movements of her slender fingers, always busy with some form of needlework; the orderly management of the household (Maud was never disorganized)—its punctual mealtimes, its menus carefully planned for two weeks ahead, its snowy linen piled in the closet. They remember the careful provisioning—the two turkeys, four geese and six ducks frozen for winter use, the four pork hams and one "beef ham" (Island terminology) cured and dried for summer meat, the keg of mackerel, box of codfish and six bags of potatoes ordered from the Island each fall.

They were amused by the little boys, restless in church, firmly marched out by their mother after adequate warning;

by Chester's habit of sliding off his chair during family prayers and producing his *Amens* from beneath the table; the little black stick Maud used to rap the boys' knuckles when they needed disciplining. They recall her love of gardening, and the flowers with which she filled the house; her pleasure in picking wild strawberries; the tamarack gum she got from Eaton's, and chewed for the sake of her teeth. They were proud of her interest in the Hypatia Club, the Uxbridge cultural society of which she was honorary president for several years.

They saw a family unity that included good-natured teasing, vigorous and friendly argument, a lot of laughter (especially when the Campbell cousins came up to visit from the Island). They noticed, too, that though she wearied for her beloved Island, Maud found much to satisfy her in the rolling, open countryside of Leaskdale, with its clumps and spreads of evergreens, and its wide skies. "After a snowfall . . . she delighted in watching for the tracks of the various creatures of the woods—here finding a mouse's or a bird's print, and there a rabbit's. She searched for every new beauty nature might reveal. . . . Her conversation was frequently pointed up with 'That reminds me' and off she would go with some 'yarn' for there was always a funny side of things. Because she was witty and gay, young and old enjoyed her company. Rarely one missed hearing some tale about her beloved Island or its people."

Cats were her passion. "How dreadful it would be *not* to love a cat!" she exclaimed to MacMillan. "I wonder if all the spirits of all the pussy folk I have loved will meet me with purrs of gladness at the pearly gates?" But beneath her passion lay an inescapable sense of guilt from a syllogism embedded in her childhood conscience. Grandma and Grandpa had hated cats: Grandma and Grandpa were wise grownups: therefore it was not right to love cats. There was always a sense of shame, though adult reason denied it, in her "pleasure in pussies . . . and as for people who say they like cats 'in their place', I know all about them from that one phrase."

At the end of 1907, Maud had written of Daffy, "He's

127

everything a cat should be, except that he hasn't one spark of affection in his soul. But then somebody has said, 'The highest joy a human being can experience is *to love disinterestedly*'. *Daffy*, therefore, gives this joy to me, since I cannot hope for any return of the affection I bestow on him." Yet, as Daffy grew older, the ability to love probably grew in him. When he died in 1920 at the age of fourteen (first thought to have been poisoned, but discovered later to have been shot), he had learned to greet Maud at the gate of the Manse and precede her up the walk. "The house is haunted by him," Maud mourned, stung by her sense of personal loss when his favourite nooks, now empty, caught her eye. This beautiful creature with his coat of silver-grey fur marked with black was not a cat, but a *person*, she said: the last living link with her old life on the Island.

She was still missing Daffy a year later, but confessed that she had "catted" again, though Paddy lacked Daffy's personality. Paddy developed a superlatively fine pair of whiskers after losing his first set to scissors wielded by six-year-old Stuart—just as an earlier cat (could it have been *Daffy?*) had lost his to young Ken Macneill in Cavendish. "When they grew out again they were about twice as long and aggressive as an ordinary cat's."

Ewan Macdonald is remembered as a bit of a tease in a heavy-handed way. One member of his congregation has recalled his attempt to make Scottish oatcakes when he was alone in the Manse on one occasion; no recipe tried by Maud had succeeded in satisfying him. His subsequent chuckling refusal to illuminate the incident led to fruitless searches for remaining cakes, tracking a trail of oatmeal from kitchen to front hall and stairs. He remained silent except to say blandly that the cakes had turned out well. Months later, two of the cakes were discovered when Maud was cleaning out his bureau drawer.

A member of his flock, asking where he got those nice slippers, was told tersely, "Where I left the money." At another time, pointing through a window, he remarked to a member of his Zephyr congregation who (he must have thought) was being unduly inquisitive: "You see that pump out there? Well, you might pump that, but you can't pump *me*." Though he served diligently, the vivid personality of his wife was to be Ewan Macdonald's chief claim to distinction as a minister.

"They would argue by the *hour*," says a relative, reminiscing. "And *how* they would argue! Aunt Maud could put him down every time. She used to get impatient because he spoke very slowly, and she would be away ahead of him before he got around to his point."

A member of his Norval congregation (he moved there in 1926) recalls Ewan as a plodder. "If it hadn't been for *her*, he'd have been unmemorable. He wasn't a very good conversationalist—a bit slow, a bit absent-minded, a bit offhand. Didn't have much of a viewpoint about anything, at least you couldn't pin him down. His sermons weren't bad, though, good down-to-earth talks, and short. But *her*! Now, *she* was the one who held things together. She was the social part of it. She'd go into the church kitchen and work with the other women—and those strawberry pies of hers! And she kept the young people enthusiastic with the talks she gave and the plays she used to direct, mostly light comedies she'd adapt for the purpose. No one would ever forget Maud Macdonald."

And no one would realize the bone-weariness she suffered as she did what duty demanded. One part of her enjoyed it; one part resented its intrusions. She would write: "Sometimes I get so sick of them [mission bands, missionary auxiliaries, ladies' aids, Women's Institutes, Sunday School teachers' meetings, etc. etc. etc.] that I could hang myself on the handiest gooseberry bush rather than go to another. And yet —it's odd—it's always in prospect only that I hate them. When I get to them I find myself really quite enjoying them. I like 'making things go', having, so I have been told, a 'gift' that way. It is really only because of the inroads they make on my time that I rise up and howl occasionally." Yet she could write, "I have lost the art of living entirely. . . . It isn't right. We weren't meant to live like that." Separately, she could have enjoyed any of her current activities. All together, crammed into one life, they were too much.

Her sons were an abiding joy, at any rate during their boyhood and early teens. On a visit to Leaskdale in June 1936, when Ewan was preaching an anniversary sermon, she found pleasure and pain oddly mixed in her weekend as a guest in the Manse where she had been mistress for fifteen years. The Manse was "full of the ghosts of little boys. . . . The little lads my sons were then seemed to be still somewhere about." In a year when her boys were young men, Chester in law school, Stuart a medical student, she could hear childish laughter in the shadows, light footsteps on the stairs; baby Stuart's "ingratiating chuckle," toddler Chester's "amusing chatter"; the joyous yelling overhead—"probably a pillow-fight," as she wrote to Weber in mid-1919—when they were supposed to be going to sleep; Hallowe'en nights when the boys accompanied their cronies with masks and pumpkins, "dancing in wild abandon round a jacky-lantern on the gatepost and shrieking like tortured savages, as half-civilized man might have, eons ago, round the sacrificial fire"; the time Chester bolted after the cat in the middle of family prayers.

Perhaps, that Sunday, sitting as a visitor in her familiar pew in the small Leaskdale church, so much smaller than the church in Ewan's charge at Norval, a smile would have hovered on her lips, as she remembered the small finger pointing to a word in the hymn-book, and Stuart's voice reading carefully aloud, "Muffer, is that *God*?" at the precise moment his father's head appeared above the pulpit. And the endless questions would come ringing back:

"Mother, who were the father and mother of the first crow?

"Mother, what were pancakes when they were alive?

"Mother, is this the only world there is, *in a sense*?"

The years had become cluttered with responsibilities, to which the war had added its burden. Days that used to be filled with things one *wanted* to do were now full of "things that *have to be done*." Maud longed for the day when the boys would be older, when she could write more often to friends: write, as she hoped to do, more *serious* literature—an optimism that was never justified in her own mind. Meanwhile, she "pegged away" at her pot-boilers.

In May 1919 the problem of a sick husband was added to others that plagued her. Suffering from what local doctors diagnosed as nervous prostration, Ewan went to visit a sister in Boston, with the idea that a rest would prove beneficial. The urgency of a wire received two weeks later demanding that she come at once sent Maud flying off fully expecting to find herself a widow on arrival. Ewan had become violently ill with what Boston doctors decided was kidney trouble; it was mid-August before he felt able to travel, and November before he could take up his work again.

Maud had been able in November 1920 to make a two-week return to "the only Island there is," but this time feeling "like a ghost revisiting a world I had once lived in, with no fellow ghosts to keep me company." Of her old life, Aunt Annie Campbell was the only one left, and the house at Park Corner was "full of youngsters who call me Aunt Maud," eyeing the rings, laces and silk dresses of this fascinating and mysterious visitor from the unknown, outside world, as she had once eyed those of aunts who descended on Cavendish.

At the end of 1920 and early in the winter of 1921, she had travelled to the Ontario towns of Chatham and London to give readings from her works, an undertaking she enjoyed. From her schooldays she had been at home on the platform, and needed no time to prepare for these appearances. During the summer, the whole family motored to Prince Edward Island via Kingston, Boston and Portland, Maine, returning by a different route. The boys—Chester nine, Stuart six and "full of mischief and devilment"—had fun picnicking along the grass-bordered roads. The scenery delighted Maud as always, though she confessed that even she "really got fed up with beauty before long." But "the great grey misty breakers of Atlantic waves rolling in" as they drove up the New England coast pulled at her heart with the old tug of ecstasy that the sea could always produce.

Throughout the year she gave several more readings in a variety of places. By October 1921 she was writing that the year had been so busy she could not say she had *lived* it—

"I've just tore about and cussed!" But the rush would get worse, the pace faster, the commitments heavier. She had been "persecuted" by demands for a short autobiographical article to appear during the Canadian Book Week campaign in November. She had been "up to her eyes" in work for the campaign. In early December she travelled to Cleveland, Ohio, to give readings, and to Montreal for the same purpose later in the month.

She complained, but she continued to involve herself. She was under no compulsion to accept the invitations she deplored; acceptance of such exhausting additional demands on her time and strength was her own decision. She could have legitimately pleaded home and church responsibilities, as well as her writing, as adequate reasons for being spared the socializing she nevertheless wearily undertook. As far back as 1909 she had been "generally bored to death" when she had "had to go out to tea and attend garden parties galore . . . then I talked gossip and made poor jokes and altogether wished I were home in my den with a book or a pen." But there is no doubt she enjoyed the adulation she received, and the image of herself that appeared in the articles published about her, and her reputation as a modest woman who "doesn't seem to consider [the first movie of *Anne*] an event of more importance than the next church christening . . . a woman of personal charm and winsomeness, as broad-minded and practical as she is imaginative, with a keen sense of humor, happy in the keeping of her home and the interests of the parish . . . a mother who mothers her children personally . . . [who] does her own housekeeping with the skill and despatch of a woman trained to it."

So she took on more than she should have undertaken, and flew about with the prodigious energy her son has remarked, and complained that life was moving too fast. And there was Christmas. For Maud, carrying as it did its double load of work in home and church, Christmas became more and more a travesty of all it stood for. She resented "the annual anguish of preparations for Christmas. . . . What a commentary upon our present day civilization that foregoing sentence is." In 1926 she described the last two weeks of December as the most hateful of the year, a time of "rush and hurry and worry" with Sunday School concerts and end-of-the-year business meetings. "Can you think of Jesus on Xmas day?" Weber had asked. No, Maud could not. It had become a *horrible* day. She deplored the sending of cards on a false basis of convention—*they* sent us one last year, *we* must return one this year. But "I am as guilty as anybody else. . . . There's something terribly wrong somewhere with most things today, I fear. But I dare say I'm just getting old and tired and that's why things seem to be going to the demnition bow-wows."

She returned to the theme years later. "Isn't it *tragic* that the observance of the birthday of the Founder of the greatest religion on earth should be mainly associated with turkey and geese and plum pudding!!"

CHAPTER TWENTY-TWO

The Wheel of Things

All through the 1920s Maud was hard at work producing new books. Seven titles were published between 1921 and 1931 and none of them truly satisfied their author, except perhaps *Emily of New Moon*. Having completed *Rilla of Ingleside* and finished, as she hoped, with Anne—"I am sick of her and wonder that the public isn't too"—she was writing in October 1921 that she had "a new kind of heroine," and liked her.

"People were never right in saying I was Anne, but, *in some respects*, they will be right if they write me down as Emily." Maud certainly injected into these books incidents and dialogue and characters of her own creating, but Emily's life story—particularly in the first book (there would be three *Emily* books)—and her dedicated intention to be a writer, follow Maud's career closely. Whole chunks of her own life are embedded in the story. The letters written by the ten-year-old Emily to her dead father, as Maud wrote to her own dead mother—written, too, on the backs of letter-bills; Emily's treasured memory of her beautiful mother as she remembered seeing her lying in her coffin; the private language Emily invented, like the language with which Maud and a friend teased their excluded school chums; Emily's unfulfilled longing to wear her hair with bangs like every other girl at the time; the Murray pride in ancestry that mirrored Maud's in the Macneills and the Montgomerys. The saintly, suffering child Anzonetta Peters is there under her own name. Emily's first typewriter copied Maud's—the one that made faint capitals and would not print the letter *m* at all. Emily climbed the same steps in education as Maud did; even Maud's real-life school-teaching is the pattern for Emily's.

Maud saw her new heroine as so different and so fresh that she was affronted by Weber's reaction. "You say 'Of course *Emily* is another *Anne*'. Well, she may be, but if so I have entirely failed in my attempt to 'get her across' to my readers." Emily's background of family and tradition, she felt, was very different from "the hail fellow well met little orphan from nowhere." She could not see any resemblance "except one or two superficial ones in the stage they walk on."

She was amused, however, to read that the only character Weber thought overdrawn was the only one taken from real life—the teacher, Mr. Carpenter. Reaction by readers was almost always the same, she had found. People tended to fit the wholly invented characters to real people and were sure those drawn from real life were imaginary. Was this because life itself is crude and imperfect, she wondered?—inconsistent with our ideas of it? "Does even truth have to have a veil of illusion to make it true?"

Anne and Emily do, in fact, share many similarities. Both are orphans, both are pert, attractive, highly articulate children with a strong awareness of individuality, both strongly imaginative, both passionate in their responses. Both are in the hands of authoritarian guardians and under compulsions that often run counter to their inclination and to their well-developed sense of what is "fair." The adult inhabitants of Emily's world are more often relatives; neighbours fill the gap in Anne's world. But these adults are endowed with similar idiosyncrasies of personality—loving or severe, crusty or peculiar, forthright or withdrawn. Some reviewers thought *Emily of New Moon*, which she had dedicated to George MacMillan, was Maud's best book since *Anne of Green Gables*. It is a view shared by many readers today.

After a busy summer in 1922, she was looking forward to a "comparatively leisurely fall," but she was right to add that it would probably turn out to be unsettled and strenuous. "Fate seems to delight in mirages." Her letter to Weber, begun on September 25, was not concluded until October 22, despite her attempt to make "what someone has called a

'Herculaneum effort' to finish it." During the year she had met Nellie McClung, fellow-novelist and ardent advocate of woman suffrage, at a dinner, and liked her, with the qualification that she was "very obvious and lacked subtlety" in a speech that was good until the absence of any real ideas became apparent. She also met the redoubtable Mrs Pankhurst at a Business Women's Club luncheon, and saw only a sweet, tired, gentle face, "like some Presbyterian elder's wife with nothing more strenuous to do than run a village Women's Missionary Society"; it was hard to picture her smashing windows and being forcibly fed in Holloway Prison. Two weeks in Muskoka in the summer were a prelude to a worrying autumn during which the Macdonalds were mixed up in a lawsuit after a car collision the previous year. They lost the suit. And had she said she expected a quiet restful fall? "Humph!" said Maud.

Hardly anyone at Leaskdale or at Norval fails to mention, with a laugh, that "Mr. Macdonald must have been the world's worst driver"—even when he drove a horse and buggy. "Oh dear! He'd dither along, veering all over the road, nearly into the ditch sometimes, hitting every pothole, stopping and starting with a jerk—yes, Mr. Macdonald was no driver!"

In 1918, when they bought their first car, a five-passenger Chevrolet, Maud became a back-seat driver, not without some justification. "I content myself with poking Mr Mac in the back with my parasol if I think he's going more than 20 miles, and saying 'Beware' in a sepulchral voice when I see him preparing to turn a corner." Maud would be involved in her share of car accidents, some of them not Mr Mac's fault; but there were many minor mishaps. "We ran over and killed [a dog] on Yonge St. this summer," Maud mourned.

In October 1923 a letter from the secretary of the Royal Society of Arts of England informed Maud that the Council had invited her to become a Fellow—the first Canadian woman to be so honoured. Maud had now become the kind of "distinguished guest" for whom audiences waited "with some trepidation," and who were astonished and relieved to find her" a comely, comfortable looking lady" with whom the years had dealt kindly. "She quickly made herself at home," said one reporter with relief, "and ere many minutes we were comfortably seated about a cheery fire talking like old friends."

She was an adept at putting people at ease, partly from her own natural good manners, partly because courtesy and kindness were right and proper qualities in a minister's wife. But her pleasant demeanour could be misleading, and the tight self-control she exercised sometimes exhausted her. When Canadian poet Bliss Carman, whose work she had admired, disappointed her by his reputed snobbishness, she commented: "If *I* snubbed as they deserve nine out of ten of the people who plague and drain me with their inanities and ineptitudes, I would have a reputation for snobbishness too. As I have learned to suffer fools gladly I escape this imputation: but I sometimes think the cost is too high." Her greatest scorn was always reserved for the people who "know it all." She had no use for snobs.

She needed the rejuvenating, revitalizing power of the Island to restore her spirit. She went back in the summer of 1923 to a shock of amazement that she could have forgotten how lovely it was. "Such fields of daisies and clover! Such sunsets and twilights and fir woods, such blue majestic oceans, such provocative alluring landscapes. Oh, I felt that I *belonged* there—that I had done some violence to my soul when I left it." Perhaps she had. She writes often like a woman thrust out of Eden. In an apologetic note to Mac-Millan in February she had written, "I am as usual very busy —too busy. I haven't time to savor life at all—caught in the 'wheel of things' as *Kim* says. If I were not a coward I think I could better matters. But I am."

Was she never tempted to quit the rat race, escape from the Wheel of Things, persuade Ewan into early retirement, find, perhaps, her dream retreat and live comfortably on the more than sufficient earnings from her pen? Once in 1922, blessedly and miraculously alone on a Muskoka holiday, she peopled an imagined island with her nearest and dearest and dreamed a life of utter contentment. Fourteen years later she would write that "wisest Fate" had always said "no" to her longing to own an island. "I wonder if Fate is so very wise. Sometimes I am tempted to think she is blind and foolish!"

She spoke sometimes wistfully of another visit to England whose literature, in which her early education was rooted, had laid its spell upon her; but she never went back, and Europe seems never to have called to her. Did her driving sense of duty compel her to the frantic pace she clearly resented? For some months in the winter and spring of 1923-24 Ewan was ill with what Maud described as "neuritis and neurasthenia," and for a while she had feared that he would have to resign. She was now into Emily III (*Emily's Quest*); she had found Emily II (*Emily Climbs*) "a bit of a bore," as she always did with sequels. As in earlier days, when she had deplored the necessity to hitch her story to a moral if she hoped to sell it, she regretted the convention that required a "flapper" to be depicted not as she really was, but as a "sweet insipid young thing . . . to whom the basic realities of life and reactions thereto are entirely unknown. *Love* must scarcely be hinted at." Nevertheless, she wrote, "I can't afford to damn the public. I must cater to it for a while yet."

She was back in Prince Edward Island for two weeks in June, this time for a sad occasion: the death of Aunt Annie Campbell, taken from the home "that was the wonder castle of my childhood" and the house in which she had been married. Aunt Annie had "left the world a very much colder place." But at the end of July, Maud made a journey that reached to her heart and stayed in her memory—a family motor trip to Kentucky's awesome Mammoth Cave. The experience impressed her so deeply that many pages of her letters to both pen-friends were given to describing it.

Although throughout their years of friendship, quite long gaps developed in what Maud and MacMillan called "real" letters, they were always in touch with quick notes, gifts, packages of clippings. At the end of August 1924, Maud had been horrified to find that two years had passed since her last "real" letter. "But a friendship as old and well-tried as ours should be able to stand alone without being propped up with apologies." She then started on a massive catching-up chronicle that went off in five parts, ending in October and totalling seventy-four pages. Much of this was taken up by her account of the trip to Mammoth Cave, probably taken straight from her journal, as she wrote to Weber in almost identical words.

Everything about the trip was memorable, even its disasters. They got lost in Detroit. Maud thought there could be no worse hell than to be a traffic cop in Detroit (just think, she told Weber, "when we began exchanging letters there wasn't a single 'traffic cop' in the United States!"). They met bed-bugs in Hicksville, Ohio; they found Indiana monotonous—mile after mile of little villages with hanging baskets, though Maud would never forget the fireflies and the "cold elusive night smells." The red roads of Kentucky, "bright island red," filled her with nostalgia. There was a terrible, endless detour, forty-five miles of dust and potholes. But the cave itself cast a spell on her. She "would be its prisoner forever." Though children and chatter destroyed some of the magic, it was the sort of place to which her imagination could instantly respond. She longed to go through it alone, or "with a kindred spirit."

In the cave costume of jacket and bloomers, each person in the group of fifteen carrying a lantern, they fumbled their way in semi-darkness, strung out along the bank of a black sullen stream in Stygian gloom—"the original Styx couldn't be Styxier"—winding up flights of rock stairs, or "flickering through stately palaces of eternal night" that echoed to the sounds of bells rung by the guides. Maud had expected to find the cave damp and mouldy, and was surprised by the steady fifty-four-degree temperature at three-hundred-odd feet underground, and by the "great wind" that met them at the entrance gates. Along the first route of five and a half miles they passed through a series of caves connected by passages, "great shadowy mysterious avenues, winding stairs of solid rock, narrow, tiny slits": the guides flung up blazing balls of cotton waste to demonstrate the vastness. The boys loved the queer animal shapes of the limestone columns, but for Maud it was not altogether a holy place. "The old gods of the underworld rule it."

The second route of three miles was even grander. In the Star Chamber, with all flares extinguished, came a strong feeling of night sky overhead. Then, after "absolute darkness," the lanterns lit by the guides turned the crystals above them into stars, and dawn noises were introduced: a man chopping wood, cattle lowing, the sound of dogs and cats. Maud sensed the touch of some unfathomable power; felt that she had left a little of herself behind, that it might not be safe to return. "Suppose it kept too much of you?"

Returning home, they were granted a spectacle put on by the gods at Niagara, where for half an hour the worst storm in thirty-seven years flashed over the unlighted Horseshoe Falls, a "ghostly shimmering, blue-white gleam of almost constant lightning, while athwart the mist tore zig-zags of living flame, as if some god were amusing himself by hurling thunder bolts into the abyss." It made the floodlit American falls look tawdry.

Maud Montgomery's body has returned to her beloved Island, where it rests in Cavendish cemetery just across the road from the site of the Macneill homestead. In the background is the Green Gables house in P.E.I. National Park. Green Gables, however, is no longer visible from the cemetery; in the years since this picture was taken the trees in between have grown up to obscure the view.

Green Gables is a magnet for tourists and golfers. Located in Prince Edward Island National Park a few hundred yards from the site of the old Macneill homestead, the house is surrounded by the golf course.

Anne's *unfailing charm has delighted audiences in stage, screen and television adaptations. Above, a still from the 1934 movie starring Anne Shirley.*

Mary Miles Minter starred in the 1919 movie version.

A scene from the smash hit musical first produced by the Charlottetown Festival in 1965. A hardy perennial at Charlottetown, the show had a triumphant national tour in 1967, represented Canada at Expo 70 in Osaka, Japan, and visited Broadway in 1971.

Canadian actresses Kim Braden (above) and Barbara Hamilton (below) in the 1975 BBC serial Anne of Avonlea, *a sequel to the popular dramatization of* Anne of Green Gables *first broadcast in 1972 and since re-broadcast.*

Some of the many languages into which L. M. Montgomery has been translated: clockwise from top left, Anne of Windy Willows *in Japanese,* Magic for Marigold *in Dutch,* Rilla of Ingleside *in Norwegian, and* Emily of New Moon *in Finnish*

Montgomery Hall, the student residence of what used to be Prince of Wales College, honours Maud's memory at her old school in Charlottetown.

Christened in 1969, the Lucy Maud Montgomery *was later switched to the Newfoundland crossing.*

Fame takes many guises, even the final hole on the golf course at Prince Edward Island National Park.

Perhaps the ultimate form of official accolade,
this stamp was issued on May 15, 1975.

CHAPTER TWENTY-THREE

An inadequate spoonful of wine

Norval, Ontario, "is a pretty little village in the valley of the River Credit, which flows just behind the Manse," wrote Maud to Ephraim Weber in July 1926. "We are on a high-way midway between Toronto and Guelph—about 28 miles or so from either place."

In February that year, Ewan had been "called" by the congregations of the Norval and Union charge, and had decided to accept, partly because of the disruption in Leask-dale caused by the recent union of some of the Presbyterian congregations with the Methodists and Congregationalists to form the United Church of Canada. After so many years in Leaskdale, Maud found "roots that have been rooted as long as that are not pulled up without pain." And she preferred to forget "the *dreadful* month of packing, moving and un-packing." Next time, she thought, she would just set fire to everything—"it would be simpler." But once settled, she entered into community life with all her old vigour and interest. The Manse was bigger than Leaskdale's, with large airy rooms, high ceilings, and in a charming location. Behind the house the ground runs down to the little river that winds back into country more wooded and steeper than Leaskdale's open hills. The property covers nearly one and a half acres; the church, opened in 1879, has curved pews, and seats about two hundred and fifty, its floor sloping toward the pulpit, the choir and the pipe organ.

Maud was now the author of fourteen published books, including the unauthorized *Further Chronicles of Avonlea*

141

and a book of verse, *The Watchman & Other Poems* (1916). She had also seen the first of two filmed versions of *Anne of Green Gables* (in 1919), and found it disappointing. Though "the photography was beautiful," the atmosphere was not right, New England was not Prince Edward Island, skunks and the American flag were not part of the Island scene, and Mary Miles Minter, who played the lead, was not "my gingery Anne." None of her books so far had truly satisfied its author, who still awaited a day when she could tackle something "serious." What she had in mind was a clan story set in the Maritimes. Knowing clan life "from A to Z" because of the Macneills, Montgomerys and Simpsons in her own background, she felt competent to tackle the theme. The difficulty would be to make it come *alive*, she thought—to get the comedy and tragedy equally balanced. But life at present was too rushed to attempt such a work. She had, however, ventured on a book directed to adults. *The Blue Castle*, out in August 1926, was set, for once, not in Prince Edward Island but in the Muskoka district of Ontario. Though she meant it for adults, it was not what she thought of as a serious attempt at a novel, "merely an amusing (I hope) little comedy." She dedicated this book to Ephraim Weber.

It was hardly a comedy, though enlivened by Maud's talent for depicting robust and pithy characters. It remains a charming and vigorous story: maybe an allegory of Maud's own frustrations, her yearning to live a secluded life in an enchanted natural setting, away from the strains and stresses of a people-encumbered existence, in total harmony with a kindred spirit. Through plot twists and coincidences, its heroine found all her problems solved in the end. Maud would always choose to write happy endings, though she allowed her sense of reality to strew the path of her characters, as in life, with problems physical, circumstantial and emotional, before she allowed them their heart's desire.

As an author of books about girls and therefore expected to be knowledgeable and understanding about youth—perhaps also because of her reputation as a successful worker in the Young People's Guilds—Maud was often asked for an opinion on the youth of the day, particularly girls. "I, alas, have nothing but sons. So what do I know about the problems of daughters?" she asked *Chatelaine* when that magazine requested an article. "[But] I was a girl once myself and have, I believe, managed to retain, even till now a very vivid recollection of what I was, and what I wished to be and how far and why I failed." Reporters who continually demanded to know "What is your opinion of girls of this so-called fast age?" were told "Just as good as those of any other generation. There is a certain proportion of 'high-fliers' in every generation—the ages do not differ radically. Girls are freer to express themselves now. The pressure is off; that is about all the difference there is between our girls now and those of a bygone day."

Maud had already portrayed the madcap, irreverent, convention-flouting girl in several of her books, notably in Ilse Burnley, Emily's closest friend: a wild girl who nonetheless had the right instincts. She wrote the article for *Chatelaine*, published in the March 1931 issue. It was, in fact, a sound piece of common sense, advising mothers to remember their own young days.

Yes, the young *were* selfish: "Just as the middle-aged of today are selfish; just as the old are selfish—and always have been." Yes, the young *were* thoughtless. "Naturally. You have to learn to think. Nobody is born thoughtful." Youth takes itself seriously. *"Never laugh at her.* Don't blow her little candles out. . . . I have forgiven the people of my youth who advised me and scolded me and lectured me. But I have never forgiven the ones who laughed at me." And "You should respect her personality and never try to force her confidence." Again, "Don't make too many things charming because of a taboo. Especially boys, who are quite charming enough without that to Sweet Sixteen. Don't let your girl pass into womanhood with nothing but starved or stolen youth behind. . . . If she hasn't a beau or two in her 'teens how on earth is she ever going to learn to manage the men?"

Excellent advice, echoing with the frustrations of her own youth. But in private Maud was less tolerant of youth. Over the years she had had long and spirited discussions on the subject with Ephraim Weber, who since 1917 had been a reluctant teacher in Saskatchewan schools. To cheer his pessimistic appraisal of the doltish minds of his pupils, she expounded an argument equally pessimistic—that today was no different from ages past: there had *never* been more than a few minds capable of being educated. So why should he worry?

In 1909, Weber had made a vital decision—to improve his education further and try teaching again, encouraged to do so by Annie Campbell Melrose, the Didsbury schoolteacher whom he married on Christmas Day of that year. Accordingly, he enrolled in the Normal School at Calgary, but found the brief period of teaching that followed as uncongenial as he had back in Waterloo County, Ontario. He therefore set his sights higher, returned to Ontario with his wife, and registered at Queen's University in Kingston for a course leading to the degree of Master of Arts in modern languages. Summer school teaching helped his finances, and he graduated three years later. After a year at Queen's as tutor in German, he spent two years at the University of Chicago, working toward a degree of Doctor of Philosophy. But various difficulties intervened, among them the war and its anti-German bias that shrank classes in German studies and made German texts often inaccessible. He also suffered a great disappointment in finding that months of research for his thesis was rendered pointless by the work of an earlier scholar. Though he acquired a reputation as a scholar, the higher degree escaped him. He could do little other than return to teaching in Saskatchewan. For sixteen years, until he retired in mid-Depression at the age of sixty-three, he taught school—despondently for the most part, although he was rewarded by the success of many of his students.

"My friend, you are growing old," Maud told him toward the end of 1922, replying to a dejected comment about the boy and girl of today. Every generation had said the same thing. "Adam and Eve said that when Cain and Abel were about sixteen. I say it, whereby I avow myself your contemporary. Eheu! Times—manners—morals—customs are not what they were! The present age is degenerate. The boys and girls are not as we were—sage, sensible youngsters that we always were!

"Oh, dear sir, youth is the same in every century. In some it is more rigorously repressed than in others but—underneath the repression it is *the same*—foolish until years teach it bitter wisdom, rebellious until life teaches the futility of rebellion, cocksure until innumerable mistakes have humbled it, selfish and indulgent and hungry—until when—alas, I fear till the grave closes over it. We do not change much; we only grow weaker and wearier."

It was partly herself she was mocking. "Thus saith the Preacher," she ended ironically.

Maud was an odd mixture of realism and idealism, of profound scepticism and undaunted optimism. Weber found it hard to free himself from disillusionment: Maud armoured herself by coming to terms with it. "I suppose our discussion on present day youth gets us nowhere," she was writing a year later, "and might as well be closed. . . . You see youth *en masse*, in the raw, with all its disagreeable qualities intensified by the companionship and backing of its mates. I see it only in my rural environment, toned down by the older people among it and bridled by the conventions that are always to a certain extent in force wherever many older people are. When you meet your pupils out in the society of older people, are they quite as crude and crass and raw and bumptious as they are taken in bulk in your classroom? I agree with you that the present day parent is largely responsible for the shortcomings of our youth. I don't know whether the parent should be blamed too much. The pace of to-day leaves a father and mother too little time for training their children properly. There have been fool parents in all ages who believed their offspring faultless and refused to back up the teacher. I was 'up against' several of these when I taught school thirty years ago. I have worked for twelve years in our Young People's Guild here and I can honestly say that I see no difference between the boys and girls of Leaskdale and the boys and girls I mingled with in my teens. Some of them are stupid and silly and crass. So were some thirty years ago."

She was willing to concede that conditions in the Canadian West might be more lawless, less restrained. But "the evil will right itself in time. And I doubt if teaching school was ever anything but a nerve racking job in any period of the world's history, or if any more than a few pupils in any school repaid the labor expended on them or were keenly interested in study for its own sake."

They were back to the subject three years later. "Teaching has some abominable things about it," Maud agreed, but she did not agree with putting the blame on modern conditions: to some extent contradicting her statement that today's pace had created problems for parents. "I think teaching all down through the ages has been pretty much the same. Only, of course, there are *more* students now when everybody 'goes to High School'. And equally of course I *don't* believe this universal 'education' of everybody is the blessing in practice that it is in theory. To me much of the 'education' of today is like an inadequate spoonful of wine in a glassful of water. The miracle of Cana is not repeated, and the good common thirst-quenching water is spoiled.

"Why ask 'how can we get our pupils to *see* their faults?' You can't. Nobody can. One of the troubles of present day education is that [it] isn't education . . . *a-tall*. It's simply a pouring-in. And why worry because one jug holds a quart and another only a pint. And that most receptacles are sieves, holding nothing at all. Be wise. Just keep on pouring, since pour you have to—and be thankful you have something to pour. Think of the teachers (hundreds of them) who haven't.

"I think 'examinations' are outworn relics of mediaevalism. . . . Why not let everyone go on through every grade? When they get out into the world *it* will examine them very thoroughly and grade them accurately and with no chance of appeal. It may grade (and rightly) some who would have failed to 'pass' the examinations. It may cast out (equally rightly) some who would have made high marks."

Her views were deeply entrenched. She was impatient with those who wasted opportunities, who were incapable of benefiting from the advantages so generously made available to them. Her own passion for learning, her delight in the subtleties of words, her unquenchable curiosity, all made her intolerant of those whose laziness or inattention lost them the reward they could have had. She saw no virtue in pushing it at them. But she saw no advantage in letting such stupidity sour her soul, as Weber seemed to have done, and she found his complaints tiresome. "I have always enjoyed his letters," she told MacMillan, "but of late years the attitude of carping criticism to everything—the aims, politics, schools, etc. etc. etc.—of the age—into which he has allowed himself to drop has rather spoiled them for me. I am heartily glad the years have not brought such a doubtful gift to *you.*"

Weber's despair over his students' uncaring attitudes came from an urgent desire to share with them his own deep delight in culture. Their failure to respond he assumed as his own failure to inspire—as if a key existed to open closed minds but he lacked the ability to find it. One senses that his letters to Maud recorded a personal dismay directed more at what must be *his* fault than at *their* limited capacity. When he found an exceptional student, no teacher could give more of himself in guidance, encouragement and friendship. One beneficiary of his kindness was Wilfrid Eggleston, later to become one of Canada's leading journalists and professor of journalism at Carleton University in Ottawa, who has recorded his respect and gratitude to Weber in his autobiography. Maud's impatience with her friend's despondent letters was her own way of handling the same kind of disappointment.

As late as the end of 1927 she was still sparring with Weber, insisting that education should be the privilege of those only who yearn for it, pursued neither for reasons of parental pride, nor for employment opportunities that required paper qualifications. Learning for its own sake was the important thing; no point in worrying about those who didn't care. And anyway, a thought: who would there be, if *all* students were bright and receptive, to do the dull, drab, prosaic, necessary work of the world?

She concluded in disgust: "And an Ontario law *compels* all children to go to school until they are sixteen! It is to laugh!"

CHAPTER TWENTY-FOUR

Realm of
the spirit

In Maud's emphatic elitest theories and Weber's deep pessimism lay a clue to their personalities. Maud was the realist, Weber the idealist. Bruised by frustrations and disappointments, Maud found her escape in the realm of imagination, of humour, of nostalgia: in matters of daily living she accepted disillusionment. She was armoured against things-as-they-are by her ability to live an inner life of mind and spirit in a land of things-as-they-should-be. "Whatever *real* life I have lived has been in the realm of the spirit," she wrote in April 1929.

Her young heroines find their fulfilment in soul-satisfying relationships: not necessarily in success through money or fame, but through perfect communion of the spirit with the right people, in the right environment and the right niche in life, though they often have to suffer before gaining their Promised Land. Jane Stuart (*Jane of Lantern Hill*) had to endure an unendurable old grandmother before finding a father after her own heart and reunited parents. Maud herself made the best of what she had, but in her private letters she sometimes writes like a woman short-changed by life, despite her public success.

Nevertheless, her rich endowments of spirit and imagination were, she must have realized, compensation enough—or almost. Who, with that intense love of beauty, could not be grateful for such a refuge from the slings and arrows? In her mid-fifties, when she was "so tired I didn't want to go on living," she went outside just before preparing for bed, and experienced "one of the rare splendid moments" of her life, hearing the wind sing "in that garden of the wild gods up on the hill called 'Russell's pines' by prosaic people. *Some* Spirit moved there—my soul caught its call and stood mute and rapt as in some vast temple of the night."

And who, with Maud's sense of humour, could not find relief in comedy from darker moods? No wonder Leaskdale folk caught her laughing to herself as she wrote: describing, perhaps, the frigid politeness with which an aspiring Emily and the successful editor she is interviewing suffer the madly destructive living-room romp of an uninhibited dog each believed to be owned by the other; or picturing Aunt Frances, refusing an aspirin to relieve a headache and "still enduring God's will in her bedroom"; or embedding a whole world of shocked folk-morality in one amber sentence: "How would you like to die in your sleep and go before your Maker in *pyjamas*, Patricia?"

She had another refuge—her lifelong personification of inanimate objects, a trait shared by her youthful heroines: the child in her flower-girl finery who runs upstairs to comfort a weekday dress for temporary neglect; the little girl who ached for the lonely, tumble-down house that needed to be loved and lived in; Emily saying goodbye to her trees—"to the Rooster Pine and Adam-and-Eve . . . to the spider crack in the kitchen window—to the old wing chair—to the bed of striped grass—to the silver birch-ladies."

And of course, for Maud, there was also the intoxication of words and phrases. "Why have some lines of poetry a potent and indescribable influence not conditioned by their merit?" she asked, quoting a verse by Felicia Hemans that always made her shiver with profound delight:

> "The sounds of the sea and the sounds of the night
>   Were around Clotilde as she knelt to pray
>   In a chapel where the mighty lay
>   On the old Provençal shore."

Did her strange response go deep "to some former life and some intense moment in that life?" She was stabbed "suddenly and piercingly" with memories of her own gulf shore, by Milton's lines "odours from the spicy shore of Araby the blest." And, she asked Weber, "Were you ever haunted by a couplet of verse for no seeming reason?" For instance;

"The little dog-angel's eager bark
Will comfort his soul in the shivering dark. . . ."

There could be worse things, she thought, than jolly little ghost-dogs. And—having just heard an owl hooting in the pines—could you call an owl anything but *owl*, she wondered? or a frog anything but *frog*? such a "funny, dear, charming word."

And of course, there was always *wonder*. Maud never out-grew wonder. Not too many years off sixty, she was marvelling at a delicate greenfly that had alighted on her hand. "What Power made it so lovely for only me to see?" And why, she asked ruefully, did that same Power also make so many hideous humans and so many bitter and ugly human lives? "Why???"

There were other puzzles, on the lighter side, and eternally fascinating to her agile mind. She compiled a list of questions she would ask the famous dead, and tossed them for comment to both Weber and MacMillan.

St Paul: *What* was your thorn in the flesh?

Pilate's wife: What did you dream of the Nazarene?

Queen Elizabeth: Were you, or were you not, secretly married to Robert Dudley?

Mary Queen of Scots: Did you know about Darnley's murder?

The Man in the Iron Mask: Who were you?

Charles Dickens: Was Edwin Drood really murdered or not?

Homer: Was there only one or half a dozen of you?

Beatrice: Did you know Dante loved you, or did you care?

Mona Lisa: What are you smiling at like that?

Abraham: Just why did you leave Ur?

Vashti: Were you ever sorry you didn't obey Ahasuerus?

Judas Iscariot: Why did you really betray him?

Weber returned a list of his own:

Beethoven: How did you create those symphonies with a stone-deaf ear?

Brutus: Were you ever sorry you stabbed Caesar?

Hamlet: Which of all the theories about you is right?

Bishops Ridley and Latimer: Is it true that in getting burned to death, the nerves are soon seared to insensibility, then easy dying?

Lucy Gray: "What became of you when you got to the middle of the bridge?

Maud too wanted to know about the fate of Lucy Gray. "The awful intriguing mystery of that phrase, 'And further there were none,' haunted me all through childhood." Oddly enough, the shadow-Lucy who had lived behind the glass doors in the Cavendish parlour had never been associated in Maud's mind with Wordsworth's mysterious lost child.

At Norval, Maud's forceful personality was making the same impact as at Leaskdale, especially—as before—on the young people; and whatever may have been her opinion about the mental level of those she worked with, and their possible capacity for receiving higher education, no one was ever hurt or slighted by Maud Macdonald. The ability to feel superior about *something* is a necessary and important part of self-esteem, and Maud had much about which to feel superior. Yet she never hurt anyone, or made anyone feel less than important.

"Last winter I had some pleasure and a great deal of worry training a group of young people to give a play," she wrote in December 1927. Norval people remember the plays she directed with as much pleasure as Leaskdale people do. "Those plays she put on were a tremendous hit everywhere. The group used to give a performance at several different places—in church basements, school halls—and the proceeds would be split between the Norval group and the host community." From the first year's performance they made $500.

Careful as she was in choosing her plays (mostly light comedy), Maud sometimes was faced by the kind of criticism that always revolted her. In one play, the part of a woman who had to climb through a window was given to a boy to forestall adverse comment about an inevitable and unseemly display of leg and underwear. The forethought did not protect her from the scandalized disapproval of a minister in the audience that a *minister's wife* should be responsible for such an outrageous impropriety. "Ah, but you must remember," Maud flashed back, "that it *isn't* the minister's wife who directs this play, it's L. M. Montgomery." And it was L. M. Montgomery who would pillory this kind of thinking in the biting little sketches—sometimes no more than one-sentence portraits—that are scattered through her pages. The mean-spirited and the narrow-minded got short shrift from Maud.

It was Maud Macdonald who sat decorously in the pew each Sunday, who attended church meetings, church socials, church bazaars, taught in Sunday School. But it was L. M. Montgomery who was writing: "I don't number public prayers as necessary. I don't care for any kind of public prayers, not even in a church. These are nearly always farces and generally unpleasing farces." It was L. M. Montgomery who felt that perhaps "a *little* evil is necessary to give spice to existence. . . . Wouldn't it be a frightfully tasteless world if there were absolutely no evil?" It was L. M. Montgomery who agreed that historic Christianity was "ghastly," and religion condemned if "by their fruits ye shall know them": who, writing of the United Church a year after it was established in Canada, said, "Personally, I really believe the day of the church is done. . . . But—a tree that took 2000 years to grow will be a long time a-dying, and I think both United and Continuing and all other churches will function for centuries yet before they finally 'peter out.' "

Until Ewan's car crash in 1920, when he had collided with the Sunday School superintendent of the Methodist Church in Zephyr, he had been all in favour of church union. Losing the subsequent lawsuit soured him on Methodists, and consequently on having any part of the United Church when it was set up. Maud had no high opinion of the new church, though "I know little of it, being of the continuing Presbyterians, thank God." It was not the birth of a new church, but the wedding of a couple of old churches too old to have offspring. "Many United Church friends are already bitterly disappointed. They say it is going to be a bureaucracy, ruled by a few at the top. . . . A too big church is *not* a good thing. It becomes clumsy and unwieldy. . . . It is no use to say that people want a church for a 'social community centre'. They don't—not to the extent of sacrificing for it and paying for it, anyhow. If . . . Jesus of Nazareth is shelved, then the church will crumble, for he was her 'one foundation' in whatever sense you take it. If the new church 'tries experiments' I fear they are foredoomed to failure. People can get moving pictures and dramatics without keeping up a church to get them. They want something else and if a church cannot give it, it may as well close its doors."

By seeking a false and fictitious strength in uniting, Maud continued, the two groups were only propping each other up "and hoping to find in numbers what they have lost in quality. Well, we—or our descendants—will see."

Twenty years before, Maud had written: "I call myself a Christian, in that I believe in Christ's teachings and do my poor best to live up to them. I am a member of the church believing that with all its mistakes and weakness it is the greatest power for good in the world and I shall always do what I can to help its cause." And "the idea that Christ must have been a wilful impostor if he were not divine does not disturb me . . . it does not disturb me to believe that he, in common with most great teachers and reformers, had an element of fanaticism—for want of a better word—in his character."

Perhaps it is significant that Maud wrote more often of *gods* than of God: she never quite escaped the spell of *Zanoni*, all beauty and terror and magic, hinting at indescribable, supernatural grandeur of soul and spirit in a universe of total knowledge and wisdom. It was as if she had sometimes caught "a glimpse of the enchanting realm beyond—only a glimpse—and heard a note of unearthly music." She had been too thoroughly repelled by the stark severity of the Presbyterianism with which she had been indoctrinated to feel other than revulsion from a strict belief in its tenets: even *her* imagination, trying to conjure up Marie Corelli's view of angels as "creatures shaped of rainbow light" was defeated by her Sunday-School-paper version of angels "wearing a sort of nightgown with big goosy-looking wings branching out from their shoulders and a mop of untidy hair streaming over their backs." She would hold fast to the church as the most powerful agency through which weak and wavering humans could be directed to ethical and moral behaviour, but she found her spiritual ecstasy and the answer to many of her questions elsewhere. Maud returned again and again, moth-like, to reincarnation: half-believing, but unable to find a firm and totally satisfying answer.

"That idea of the immortality of *character* never appealed to me. Too few of our characters would *bear* immortality. I would *like* to believe in a personal immortality but find it difficult. I *do* believe that the spark of life within us we call the spirit is immortal and indestructible and that when it is released by the decay of the body it joins again the great tide of life that flows through the universe until its next 'incarnation'—which happens, I believe, whenever some fit organism seizes it and holds it. And so on in unending cycles. But I can't believe much as I would like to that it retains aught of our memories and personalities. However, all our curiosity will be satisfied some day—or there will be no curiosity."

Many books, re-read, made her wonder how she could ever have enjoyed them. But re-read in 1924, *Zanoni* kept the old enchantment "as subtly delightful as of yore—as full of romance, inspiration, suggestion, gramarye." Had MacMillan read it?—if not, she would send him her copy. She quoted sonorous, turgid sentences to MacMillan in pure remembered delight. . . . "Child of heaven and heir of immortality, how from some star hereafter wilt thou look back on this ant-hill and its commotions. . . .Ho, young Chaldean, young in thy countless ages, young as when, cold to pleasure and to beauty thou stoodest in silence on the old fire tower and heard the starry silence whisper to thee the last secret that baffles death, fearest thou death at length?"

Zanoni gave up his immortality for mortal love and vanished at death into the eternal life-stream. Only Mejnour, the emotionless Master Mystic, retains his personality. How did *Zanoni* ever find its way into a strict Presbyterian home in the remote little village of Cavendish?

CHAPTER TWENTY-FIVE

A squirrel
running...

At the end of 1927, Maud was more than ever caught on the Wheel of Things. She had no time, she would never catch up: "there's something terribly wrong somewhere with most things today, I fear." She really needed a secretary, but was sure she could not find one who would consent to live in such a quiet little spot as Norval. Some of her home duties had decreased, however, as the boys grew older. Only Stuart, now twelve, was at home: Chester, at fifteen, had already been a boarder at St. Andrew's School in Toronto for two years. A year previously he had been as tall as his father and wearing size sixteen clothes.

Maud had not been well this fall: in her next incarnation she hoped she would be "one of the daughters of Mary. The daughters of Martha have decidedly the worst of it!" She had been writing a series of short stories for the *Delineator* about a little girl called Marigold who found life "int'resting," but four of them would not now be published because a new editor wanted more sophisticated fiction. Maud felt let down. She had hoped that publication in the *Delineator* would have helped to advertise *Magic for Marigold*, the book made from the series in 1929. One chapter appeared in *Chatelaine* in April that year. Maud was entertained by the illustration in the Italian version, in which the hired man wore a splendid uniform, and a picture of the Virgin Mary adorned the wall over Marigold's Presbyterian bed.

But there still remained the Island, and July had been "a blissful month. . . . I have never been away. And oh, how

lovely—and lovelier—and loveliest—it was. How satisfying."
Though cars were now raising red dust on Island roads, Maud
rejoiced to find herself once again on *buggy* rides, just poking
along in no hurry to get anywhere, "past little hollows full
of scented fern, past little 'pole' gates under spruce trees, past
stone dykes hung with wild strawberries, and over looping
blue rivers and through valleys where amber brooks called—
and always the fragrance of dead fir coming unexpectedly
every little while—that fragrance which is as the wine of old
romance to me and always opens some floodgate in my soul."

During this visit to the Island, a letter to Maud from
Number Ten Downing Street gave startling proof that her
readers were not necessarily girls, or young. The Prime Minister of Great Britain, Stanley Baldwin, was travelling to
Canada to attend the diamond jubilee of Confederation.
Could he meet her? He had specifically asked the Government of Canada to include Prince Edward Island in his
itinerary. "I cannot," he wrote to Maud, "come home without
having seen the Anne country . . . I know I should be perfectly at home at *Green Gables*."

She missed him on the Island, for she had to return home
before his visit, but she "purred real loud" at the honour.
Back in Ontario, however, she received an invitation to the
Garden Party at Government House in Ottawa to meet the
Prince of Wales who, with his younger brother George (later
Duke of Kent), was also in the Dominion for the anniversary
celebrations. She found the Prince "a bored young man" and
his brother "a duck of a fellow"; and she had her chat after
all with her Ministerial fan in the grounds of Rideau Hall.

Another British prime minister would bring another purr
from Maud in the 1930s when Ramsay MacDonald told one
of her friends how much he regretted missing Prince Edward
Island on a recent visit to Cape Breton: he had always wanted
to see the Island since reading Montgomery's books.

"Oh, you read her books?"

"Yes . . . I've read every Montgomery book I could get my
hands on two and three times over."

In July 1928, Maud and Weber met face to face for the

first time, when Weber and his wife were motoring through eastern Canada. They would meet again twice, in October 1930 in the West, and in the East again in the summer of 1935. After the 1930 meeting, Weber made brief comments about her to his friend Wilfrid Eggleston, who later edited, in *The Green Gables Letters*, those written by Maud to Weber between 1905 and 1909. On her 1930 trip to the West, she gave a reading at the Battleford Collegiate (but though she described the trip to MacMillan, she did not mention meeting Weber). Weber thought "she reads well and has an impressive presence on the stage, though she is short. . . . [She] seems to be hardened both to praise and blame, though she can still appreciate appreciation. . . . She is so modest that one has to ask to learn much."

Maybe Maud was reticent in general conversation but in her letters she revealed much of herself.

She wrote to Weber in April 1929: "No, I am not dead, dumb, nor demented—though sometimes I wonder if I am not on the verge of the latter!" She had felt, she said, like a squirrel running endlessly around a wheel. A week in Muskoka in August 1928 had been almost the only happy event she could record, when she and Ewan had slept one night in a little cabin on a sandy shore. She had sat on a log in the dreamy twilight to bask in restfulness, the tree-shadows in the rose and silver water "lovelier than the trees themselves," and had got up early to watch dawn mists over the lake. But fall and winter had been a catalogue of illnesses and mishaps. Three weeks of influenza in September had been followed by a fall down some stairs in the church and a sprained arm for seven weeks, three of them in a sling. December brought a bad cold, January intestinal flu and a mysterious rash on her face, February tonsilitis. She was, she said, feeling like a demoralized dish-rag.

Stuart joined Chester at St. Andrew's in September 1928, and Maud found the house lonely, "as if someone had died . . . that dark silent room where he had slept! . . . The halls that echoed to his whistle!" She had seen much of herself in Stuart, touched when one night, with her own gift for assigning emotions to inanimate objects, he had sleepily asked to be reassured that he had set his boots together under the bed "so that they will be company for one another." And who could resist the child who hoped "if I am ever born again *you* will be born again as my mother"?

She had completed *Magic for Marigold,* and in response to a demand for another adult novel, she was collecting material for a story about an old heirloom jug. She had also got through a varied programme of reading, some of which inspired her, some disgusted her. Reading poems by Wilson MacDonald—though she found them "very beautiful"—made her sad for the lost days of great poetry.

Nor would there be any more great hymns, which "come out of a deep and fervent belief in the supernatural. Our age has lost that belief—and I do not believe it will ever return. Which is a great pity. Because mankind are lonely creatures without gods, and without gods no great hymns can be." She said she had never written a hymn and never would. Perhaps she did not remember her *Island Hymn,* or did not count it worthy of recall.

She thought free verse was simply laziness. There could be no such thing: the very essence of verse lay in its bondage to certain rules, otherwise it could be nothing but readable prose. To MacMillan she wrote disgustedly:

"I feel
Very much
Like taking
Its unholy perpetrators
By the hair
Of their heads,
(If they have any hair)
And dragging them around
The yard
A few times
And then cutting them
Into small, irregular pieces
And burying them
In the depths of the blue sea.
They are without form

And void,
Or at least
The stuff they produce
Is.
They are too lazy
To hunt up rhymes
And that
Is all
That is the matter with them."

This was the year she was reading *Exploring the Universe*, which had made her feel breathless by its scope. She felt, she said, "a little as if I would like to give up such astounding explorations and squat down in a grassy corner and play 'knifey' without thinking about the staggering processes that attend 'first fingery' and all the rest of the motions." (Strange, she mused, how such games survive, outliving dynasties and kingdoms. Children were still playing 'knifey,' a game for boys, but Maud had played it too: going through the ritual motions of her childhood, *first, second and third fingery, front-handy, back-handy, fisty, breasty, eary, nosey, mouthy, foreheady, right and left shouldery, over heady and 'shoot the pigeon'* . . .) And yet, she said, nothing in the book explained the fundamental mystery—"how, when I decided to do 'first fingery,' the decision gets from my mind to my muscles. I don't think the scientists will ever discover that. God will always keep a few secrets to himself."

Though Maud accepted the realities of ugliness in the world, she could not bring herself to portray them in her writing. Literature, to her, meant the exposition of beauty, an escape from what was all too evident and inescapable in life. Ugliness, she recognized full well, but was it necessary to fasten one's eyes on it to the exclusion of all else? Hence she was repelled by "that much be-trumpeted novel"[*Strange Fugitive*] from the pen of a new Toronto writer, Morley Callaghan, whose idea of literature "seems to be to photograph a latrine or pig-sty meticulously and leave nothing else in the picture." It was "the deadliest dull thing" she had ever tried to read. She too was aware of pigsties and latrines, but what she saw at the same time was the garden before them, the blue sky over them, the velvety pines behind them, the "misty hills of glamor beyond"—just as real, she insisted, as the latrine and the pigsty, and just as visible. She was probably visualizing the Cavendish privy in its orchard setting as she wrote.

Maud was sensitive enough to criticism of her "lack of realism" to defend her approach in public speeches. "Sunsets are just as real as pigsties," she told the Toronto Women's Press Club defiantly in 1936. Or was it less sensitivity than a blow struck against what she genuinely saw as a growing "uglification" of literature? She had been brought up on the majestic, ringing prose and poetry of the masters, from the Bible down through the ages, whose themes had been grandeur, whose canvases had shown sweeping visions. "I'm learning [Byron's] Prisoner of Chillon by heart," she had written in 1905, "because I want to remember it in the next world." Every year now she had difficulty in finding a book she thought MacMillan would like.

She did not think, as Callaghan seemed to, that you were a "sentimentalist" if you dwelt on beauty. When Weber replied that he thought the book "wishy-washy," Maud howled. "Why, you benighted Philistine! [Callaghan] thinks he is the only person writing real 'he-man' fiction in Canada!!!!"

The year 1929 was, like most of Maud's years, one of mixed pleasure and pain—"many pinpricks and some delights. Which is the common lot of humanity. Selah." Abcessed teeth had been removed in November 1928, and she had had to wear a temporary set until the following August. In December a neighbour rushed in with appalling news. There had been an accident as the radial car was proceeding to nearby Georgetown: it had collided with a snowplough and Mr Macdonald was "broken." Where? His back, his limbs, his head? A distracted Maud was getting into coat and wraps when a cutter delivered her husband, whose knees had been sprained, keeping him in bed for three weeks and at home for six. Had the accident occurred two minutes later, however, the car would have been on a bridge over the Credit River and dumped its passengers into the sixty-foot gorge below.

CHAPTER TWENTY-SIX

Fans and critics

Of Maud's most famous book, *Anne of Green Gables,* her former professor, Archibald MacMechan, wrote in 1924: "The . . . book just misses the kind of success which convinces the critic while it captivates the unreflecting general reader. The story is pervaded with a sense of reality; the pitfalls of the sentimental are deftly avoided; Anne and her friends are healthy human beings; their pranks are engaging; but the 'little more' in truth of representation, or deftness of touch, is lacking; and that makes the difference between a clever book and a masterpiece. . . . Miss Montgomery has created her public and she supplies it with what it wants. The conclusion to be drawn from Miss Montgomery's achievement is that the great reading public on this continent and in the British Isles has a great tenderness for children, for decent, and amusing stories, and a great indifference towards the rulings of the critics." All through the years that followed *Anne of Green Gables,* Maud continued to receive a massive fan mail, as English and Australian and European readers were added to her North American audience. At Leaskdale, her mail continued to arrive in bundles and basketsful, demanding some kind of acknowledgement in almost every case. "[She] maintained a voluminous correspondence," says her son, "writing by hand every fan letter reply and a detailed daily diary over 55 years."

One fan letter had been addressed to Miss Anne Shirley, care of Miss Marilla Cuthbert, Avonlea, Prince Edward Island, Canada, Ontario. One correspondent addressed Maud as "My dear long-lost uncle"—Uncle Lionel—believed by the writer to be an L. M. Montgomery who had disappeared years before. Maud was offered plot ideas by people willing to sell their own life stories for "half the proceeds." An illiterate letter in 1909 had considerably warned her against false hopes: the writer's motive was friendship only—he was a married man.

A young girl asked whether Anne kept a diary and, if so, would she publish it? An eighty-five-year-old man kept worrying that he would not live to read the next book. Years later, at a Toronto convention, a woman told Maud how she had been helped through labour pains by gales of laughter when her husband read *Anne* aloud.

In 1922, Maud was disgusted by a fan ("a male prig") who, convinced by her books that "a real Christian can still write books"—this brought a spatter of exclamation marks from Maud—"then went on to warn me my nefarious habit of marrying off my characters 'tends to lower the conception of the holy state of matrimony'. . . . I wonder if he thinks it would be better if I let them mate up without marrying . . . or sent them into convents!"

Mid-winter had seen the arrival, in one day, of eighty-five letters from Australia where, without her consent, a girl had published Maud's address. She answered them all (more than a thousand altogether dribbling in until May), but rather curtly. Probably run-down (she was also about a third of the way through her "jug" story), she had a bad attack of influenza in June 1930. The arrival of the boys for the summer vacation cheered her up: Stuart had led his class in his first two years at St Andrew's, and was already thinking of a medical career; Chester, about to enter university, had decided on mining engineering. In April 1931 his parents drove him to the "Dantean landscape and barren rocky hills" of Sudbury to work for the summer with International Nickel.

That fall, Maud had her first personal experience of broadcasting, reading a couple of poems over the air, and found she missed a live audience. The novelty of radio had hit her first in 1923, but with apprehension rather than with pleasure. "These discoveries treading on each other's heels give me a sense of weariness and *homesickness* for the slower years of old. . . . Those of us living now have to speed on with them willy-nilly. . . . And none of these things really 'save time'. They only fill it more breathlessly full."

Her winter had been the usual rush of social functions, crowded with too many events she considered useless and pointless. But she had kept up with her reading, going through Pope's *Iliad* for the first time ("a gigantic fairy tale") and not able to resist chortling to Weber that even a thousand years ago Homer was lamenting the degeneracy of modern days:
"A mighty stone such as in modern days
 No two of earth's degenerate sons could raise."
Yet her own disillusionment about modern days went quite as deep, in many ways, as Weber's.

The new book (the "jug" book) had gone off to the publisher in February 1931 with a great flurry of indecision about a title. It finally appeared as *A Tangled Web* in Canada and as *Aunt Becky Began It* in England, after going through *Aunt Becky* (absurd, said Maud, because Aunt Becky dies in the first section); *The Moon Man* ("ridiculous"); *Crying for the Moon* (didn't sound like a Montgomery book, said the publishers); *Roses of Love* or *Ribbons of Moonlight* (nice, sentimental, blue-and-pink sweet-sixteen titles, scoffed Maud, for a humorous story about middle-aged people); *The Quest of the Jug* and *The Fun Begins*. The different English title was to avoid confusion with *The* Tangled Web just published by another house.

The plot of *A Tangled Web* sounds an unpromising one to sustain a whole book, dealing with the behaviour over a full year of people who all hope to inherit a rather hideous but valuable heirloom jug. In fact, Maud managed to inject so much humour into her characters and situations, putting her finger unerringly on small foibles and small mishaps, that the interest is maintained even though the sub-plots are contrived to work out everything for everyone's best. One could find less interesting character studies than Aunt Becky's self-written obituary, which her terrified relatives feared she might actually arrange to have published:
". . . Her temper was about the average, neither worse nor

better, and did not sweeten as she grew older. She always behaved herself decently though many a time it would have been a relief to be indecent. She told the truth almost always, thereby doing a great deal of good and some harm, but she could tell a lie without straining her conscience when people asked questions they had no business to ask. She occasionally used a naughty word under great stress and she could listen to a risky story without turning white around the gills, but obscenity never took the place of wit with her. She paid her debts, went to church regularly, thought gossip was very interesting, liked to be the first to hear a piece of news, and was always especially interested in things that were none of her business. . . . She longed for freedom, as all women do, but had sense enough to understand that real freedom is impossible in this kind of a world, the lucky people being those who can choose their masters, so she never made the mistake of kicking uselessly over the traces. . . ."

And there is something richly comic in Tom Dark's acquisition of a dislocated shoulder. "The night before, as he was sitting on his bed . . . he had absently put both feet into one pajama leg. Then when he stood up he fell on the floor in what his terrified wife at first thought was a fit. Very few of the clan sympathized with him . . . they thought it served him right for wearing new-fangled duds. If he had had a proper nightshirt on it couldn't have happened."

This was the only book, apart from *The Blue Castle*, that Maud wrote for adult readers. As far back as September 1908 she had recognized her limitations, though she was not ready to give up her aspirations. "Some day I shall try to write a book that satisfies me wholly," she wrote then, but she added: "I do not think I'll ever be able to write stories for mature people." Her subsequent fan mail from adult readers gratified her but did not satisfy her sense of literary achievement. She might have been taken aback, however, to know that *The Blue Castle* would be published in 1972 for young readers in one of a series, *Canadian Children's Favourites*.

Critics continue still to differ in their assessment of her work. Desmond Pacey, writing in 1952 on *Creative Writing in Canada*, dubbed the 1910s and 1920s as "the age of brass" in Canadian literature, including Maud's name as a best-selling author of the period, although he exempted her first book from the cutting dismissal given to her later work. A. L. Phelps, a year earlier, had been more generous in *Canadian Writers*. "Coming at it freshly and with an attempt at open mindedness, to my surprise, I enjoyed some of it as a relief from the tension and self-conscious craftsmanship and experimental techniques of many contemporary works presumably much more important and widely read . . . L. M. Montgomery's work . . . is unpretentious to the point of being naive. Its innocence seems always on the edge of suggesting close cousinship with ignorance . . . of life. Yet, as one reads, the sophisticated reader is uneasily aware that the argument might turn and go in another direction. The unpretentiousness and innocence may be the kind of honest simplicity that does have life and even art in it. . . . It may be that L. M. Montgomery, one of our popular so-called mediocre story tellers, should not be dismissed too casually just because she has been popular."

Elizabeth Waterston, writing in 1966 (*The Clear Spirit*), has been more penetrating and even kinder. "[L. M. Montgomery] may . . . lay increasing claim to our attention as adult critics. . . . Writing 'for children', she could re-enact the rituals of childhood. Recreating her own remembered yearnings and anxieties, she could create a myth of the hesitant desires and worries of the virginal years. . . . Re-reading the . . . books with even a reserved acceptance of Freudian symbolism would surprise most of us. . . . Such a Freudian re-reading, besides increasing our interest in the 'Anne' and 'Emily' books, may lead to a revaluation of *The Blue Castle*, where many of the suppressed themes are directly stated."

An intelligent, educated woman of today has privately confessed that *The Blue Castle* remains one of her favourite books. So it does of this writer. The plot contrivances are incidental to the charm of the setting and the neat and witty character portraits. And there is no doubt about Maud's ability in the mind of Dr Moncrieff Williamson, director of the Confederation Art Gallery and Museum in Charlottetown, where the original manuscript of *Anne* is held. He says unhesitatingly: "*Anne of Green Gables* is an extremely sophisticated book."

CHAPTER TWENTY-SEVEN

Old books
and new views

The winter of 1931-32 was remarkable for mildness. Maud picked lettuce, cosmos, marigolds, lupins and roses in December; even in mid-January, tulips were up two inches and crocuses were blooming. At the 1931 Canadian Authors Association in Toronto she had been both bored and interested, "though whether it helped the cause of Canadian literature the gods alone know." She enjoyed several luncheons, and was saved by interesting table companions from the "boring and long-winded programs" at government-donated and city-sponsored dinners. *Interesting*, in her terms, did not always mean free from flaw. She was secretly amused (though doubtless careful not to show it) by Wilson Mac-Donald's "naiveté" as he gravely informed the group that, like Rabindranath Tagore and Walt Whitman, he never ate meat—" 'it was not fit food for genius.' " Maud, free from any pretensions to genius, "ate all the good things I could get."

There was an eighteen-month gap between her letter of December 27, 1931 (not completed until January 17, 1932) and her next dated July 16, 1933. She liked the freedom to write at will, without apology; her diary and notebooks enabled her to recall and comment on past events of importance. Personal news was limited. She was working on another book "like Anne," called *Pat of Silver Bush*. Stuart would be entering university in the fall to begin his medical education; he had been for two years junior gymnastic champion of Ontario, and the previous year placed second in the national contest at the Canadian National Exhibition (he would win the national title in September 1933). She had dropped away from Canadian Authors Association affairs and hardly saw any of the members. She was having the greatest fun with a movie camera, her gift for acting as a judge in a Kodak-sponsored international photography competition in September 1931. She was utterly entranced by the films she took on her visit to the Island in the following month—she had never wanted to be a millionaire before possessing this plaything. It was "spooky"—as if you had got out of your body—to see yourself walking and talking, feeding the cats, looking at Lover's Lane trees. Island friends flashing across the screen *must* hear you if you called to them.

But if personal news was uneventful, Maud could always find other things to write about, though not very happily. These were the years of the Depression: she had been helping to make up bales and boxes for distressed churches and institutions in western Canada (a little resentful of what she called the "crickets"—things were hard in the East too, but "we 'ants' " had managed to carry on without help). She was even sicker of the word "Dee-pression" than of the reality, she told MacMillan. Russia was looming darkly over Europe. Her own generation had seen wrenched from its pedestal and hurled to ruins everything that had been believed im-movable, "our whole world turned upside down," stirred up in a welter of doubt and confusion and uncertainty: she envied her mother and grandmother their "unchanged and practically unchanging world," when religion, politics, so-ciety, all were nicely mapped out, arranged, organized.

She had been growing gradually more despondent about the prospects for a better world, retreating into the comfort-able world of the classics, re-reading old favourites, for refuge from "modern hysterics." She saw no hope for a warless world; the pacifists had not invented any conclusive answer yet. "But then there are no longer any gods," she wrote with bitter sarcasm. "And our fathers were only mistaken old fools who didn't know beans. Why die for their ashes? Far better make fertilizer out of them."

She was turning back to older books, since "good fiction seems to have died the death"; like the man who had said " 'whenever a new book comes out I read an old one.' " In this mood she had enjoyed reading Samuel Butler's *The Way of All Flesh*—not a modern sex novel, she assured Weber, but "a mordant, ironic arraignment of everything. It's a book full of *half-truths*." Living in a world she saw as upside-down, with its traditions ripped away and its beliefs shattered, she found solace, too, in Trollope's world of fixed and unquestioned social patterns.

Recoiling from the licence of the modern novel, Maud was reading more history and biography. A new life of Charlotte Bronte by E. F. Benson enthralled her, though she thought it probably did not present the author any more truly than Mrs Gaskell's "saintly" portrait did. Charlotte, she commented, had an unenviable talent for disliking almost everyone she met—"no gift for suffering fools gladly."

She had written once to Weber, "Perhaps a *little* evil is necessary to give spice to existence—like the dash of cayenne that brings out the flavours of a salad and saves it from vapidity? Wouldn't it be a frightfully tasteless world if there were absolutely *no* evil?" It is refreshing to find the dash of cayenne in the bland flavour of the character Maud herself offered to her world. It could not be said of her that, like Charlotte Bronte, she disliked almost everyone she met; but she did not care for as many people as her manner indicated and, like her Aunt Becky, she enjoyed spicy gossip. Her private judgments were candid and not always kind, both about personal acquaintances and her literary contemporaries. Though she liked some of Wilson MacDonald's poetry, she did not like the man himself; Bliss Carman was a disappointment, Nellie McClung had no substance, Edna Jaques was "personally uninteresting." Though she had found Amy Lowell's prose "delicate and beautiful," she had been shocked to discover that "[she] is a perfect *giantess*, very masculine, *smokes, swears*." When she discovered who had designated her work as "the nadir of Canadian literature," she passed on to Weber some unpleasant gossip about the *Globe and Mail* critic William Arthur Deacon. And she was touchy about Mazo de la Roche's success, rearing up at a suggestion that *her* dominating grandmother in *Magic for Marigold* had been modelled on the Whiteoaks matriarch. Marigold and her dominating grandmother had been in the *Delineator* long before and, anyway, Maud said, she hadn't read the *Jalna* books. Did no other Canadian dare depict a dominating grandmother for the next hundred years? Had Miss de la Roche taken out a copyright on the idea?

"Dear, dear!" she had written in 1927, "the gods shouldn't come to earth at all. One can't help suspecting that they are only half-gods after all."

Her letters, like a confessional perhaps, were a safe outlet for private disillusionments: her increasing weariness, her reputation as a good mixer maintained at such a cost of energy and distaste, her treasured traditions considered unimportant in this brash new world. Perhaps, too, she had finally accepted with resignation the limits of her talent. She would not, after all, write the great book, give to the world the deathless poems that surged in her mind beyond her powers of expression. It was in another life that she had written in her journal, in her twenties: "Oh, I wonder if I shall ever be able to do anything worth while in the way of writing. It is my dearest ambition"; and from some cold boarding-house during her school-teaching years, "Oh, I love my work!" She had been wildly successful, but she had not met her own literary standards.

She was becoming a "latitudinarian," she said, as she grew older. Yet she had always been secretly a liberal thinker. Perhaps she meant her ardent idealism and optimism for the human spirit had now hardened into a vain expectation— "Why kick against the pricks?" Human nature would not change: as it had been in the days of Rameses, so it would be in 10000 A.D. A sense of being trapped—somehow betrayed by life—permeates her letters. But not until the very end of her life did she give a clue to her greatest despair.

She need not have spent herself on church duties, public appearances. Her famous-author status would have excused her from all but a token performance as minister's wife. But Maud was Maud Macdonald before she was L. M. Montgomery: latitudinarianism did not go far enough to undermine her loyalty, her view of what was right and proper behaviour.

The winter of 1933-34 was a terrible one, perhaps to pay for the mild one the year before: unbroken cold from early November until early March. Maud was beset by colds and the ceaseless effort to keep warm. Only two notes went to MacMillan in 1934, "quite the most terrible year I have ever lived." In January 1935 a massive fifty-four-page letter went off in two parts, giving more details, mostly about Ewan's health, which (Maud explained) from March until the end of the year had gone through influenza and insomnia to a complete breakdown, with nearly four months in a sanatorium, two more months at home in misery, and a month of recuperation on the Island. No wonder that Maud "staged a little breakdown of my own and for six weeks couldn't sleep or eat or work."

At the end of 1935, Ewan resigned from the ministry, and in July 1936 Maud was writing from "Journey's End" at 210A Riverside Drive, Toronto, "on a winding road on the banks of the Humber River." The house backed onto a deep ravine where pines, oaks, bracken and wildflowers delighted her. She was charmed to discover that the wind howled around the house in storms. And she was happy that both boys could now live at home again.

A new movie (this time a talkie) of *Anne* had just been released, approved in general by Maud. She liked the little actress who played Anne, whose real name was Dawn Paris. She had been using the stage name of Dawn O'Day, but thenceforth adopted the name of Anne Shirley. It made Maud feel "a bit like Frankenstein" to see the name on theatre marquees. She saw the film four times. But an enthusiastic MacMillan topped her record. "You actually went to see the Anne film seven times!" she marvelled.

Matthew and Marilla Cuthbert were "good in their own way," though Maud thought this Marilla was actually more like her own concept of Rachel Lynde. She did not like Gilbert, and "Diana was a washout." And if anyone had told her all those years ago that one day a man would *fly* across the continent to take the part of Matthew in "a moving and talking picture . . . I would have wondered why the poor prophet was being let wander about loose." The actor, O. P. Heggie, died shortly after making the picture. In 1936, when *Anne* was being shown at a local theatre, Maud's twenty-year-old maid was mystified. "But how can they put it on now?—when that man is dead?"

Probably the highlight of Maud's 1935 was her investiture by the Governor General, Lord Bessborough, with the insignia of the Order of the British Empire. Each of those to be honoured was given "a sort of hooked pin" to wear, on which his Excellency hung the medal, a handsome one in the shape of a gold Maltese Cross about two inches square attached to a richly coloured bow. The medal bore the order's legend on the front: on the back was engraved the King's monogram. It could be worn only when "a representative of the King" was present, but a miniature could be made and worn to any full-dress evening affair. Maud found herself amused by the accompanying warrant signed by the King. "I wonder if the poor man ever heard of his 'trusty and well-beloved Lucy Maud Montgomery Macdonald' before he signed it."

It was typical of Maud to notice and be tickled by the two inches of white underslip showing beneath the elegant dark blue dress of a gorgeous lady who proceeded up the long "throne" room at Rideau Hall to curtsey to the Governor General in blissful ignorance of the mishap to her clothing. Maud's own progress and curtsey, she was told by friends later, came off "nicely." She was more interested in the ceremony of dubbing the knights, a ritual much more elaborate and lengthy than that for Officers of the Order of the British Empire.

CHAPTER TWENTY-EIGHT

The gleam
and the glory

Like her Emily, Maud had felt near to the secret heart of the mystery, only a fragile veil's-width away from all the answers she would never find in church. Her gods were beauty and truth; and reality, for her, lay in her writing where, through the thoughts and actions of her characters, she could safely express unorthodoxy, hit out at remembered injustices, and re-live the joyous world of her youth. Yet in that world, her sharp eye saw the human flaws, her keen ear heard the note of protest. Few writers have better portrayed the plight of sensitive children under the authority of uncompromising adults. All her heroines are hag-ridden to greater or lesser extent by these guardians, well-meaning but obtuse: they are adolescent girls alone in a world more or less hostile, unprotected by the parents with whom they had once lived or (they passionately believed) would have lived in close and sympathetic companionship. Only Jane Stuart, of all Maud's heroines, once she had discovered her charming father—and perhaps Pat, with her happy home life at Silver Bush and full complement of parents—really escaped the tyranny of nagging adults. Anne and Emily and Marigold constantly ran head-on into the prejudices of the period in those small, infinitely important crises erupting in the daily round of life in school and home. All too well Maud understood and was able to depict the soul-destroying power of the trivial, and the incurable scars small stabs can leave. "I think the little things in life often make more trouble than the big things," said Anne with Maud's own insight.

Her books, by their very nature, are more powerful than her short stories (which she continued to write and sell throughout her life): especially those with romantic plots frequently based on the emotional reconciliation of people who had let some stupid tiff keep them apart into middle age, a theme that appealed to her romantic nature. Stories featuring children are much more successful. Maud's child characters are natural little creatures with human flaws, neither all bad nor all good, and she uses them skilfully for sly digs at absurd adult behaviour or the prim conventions of the day. The children scold each other with the virtuous morality they have imbibed from their elders.

"You ought to be ashamed, speaking of such things," says Felicity primly in *The Golden Road*, echoing sex taboos, shocked by the mere mention of the unborn children the future might bring. (Emily, too, came under fire from an outraged aunt for bringing the word *bull* into drawing-room conversation.)

"If he's converted, he oughtn't to get mad," remarks another small prig—answered philosophically by a realist, "Well, lots o' people do."

In every book the children endlessly attempt to fit the concept of a kind God to the petty tyrant their elders seemed to believe in, and to the cross old man of religious illustrations. They know that Presbyterians are the elect of God, but they wonder why the Bible had no mention of either Presbyterians or Methodists, though it did mention at least one Baptist. Ministers are sacrosanct, even when unlikable.

"A common man would be queer, but when it's a minister, it's eccentric."

"Uncle Roger says that if he had been a Roman Catholic he would have become a monk, but, as he was a Presbyterian, all he could do was to turn into a crank."

"They're going to make a minister of him. . . . He's bound to have all the fun he can before he begins to be a minister, 'cause he doesn't expect to have much afterwards."

"I don't think it's right to tell a funny story about a minister. It's not respectful."

"You shouldn't speak of the—the—*devil*". . . . "Well, that's just what Mr Scott said." "Oh, it's all right for a *minister* to speak of him. But it isn't nice for little girls."

"It's no wonder we can't understand the grown-ups," says the Story Girl, when the children's sermon contest has brought a scolding for jesting about "sacred things," "because we've never been grown-up ourselves. But *they* have been children, and I don't see why they can't understand us."

In her almost plotless books—a series of anecdotes and incidents strung on the thread of a child's journey to adulthood—Maud's strength in capsule characterization is particularly marked. She has made telling and effective use of the kind of detail every reader will recognize. Every story she was ever told, every person she met, every human situation she encountered, every phrase she read or heard, all were noted down, stored away, to be used unchanged or brought to sparkling new life by the touch of her darting imagination. Everything was the stuff of stories for Maud. Even those terrible premonitory dreams during the war were used, grafted onto the schoolteacher Gertrude Oliver in *Rilla of Ingleside*.

The inescapable power of natural beauty to haunt and compel her, the tormenting need to purge her soul of its ecstasy in verbal expression, led her often into the excesses she was able to mock through the characters she created, but could not correct in her own writing. Her purple patches, and the clichés of her romantic and frankly commercial short stories have led many critics to overlook the real flashes of insight and often wit in her characterizations, especially those of adolescent girls and crusty eccentrics.

"You're too fond of purple, Emily," the young Emily is told by a candid teacher. "Cut out all those flowery passages," was Anne's teacher's advice. "And I'd let the sun rise and set in the usual quiet way without much fuss over the fact."

But when it came to sunsets and sunrises, Maud was lost. Morning and evening were new miracles that had to be captured and recaptured on her pages. In one book alone (*Anne of the Island*), sunset after sunset trailed glory through successive pages. "The sun began to burst out goldenly now and again between the rents in the clouds, burnishing the grey seas with copper-hued radiance. . . . The perfect half hour that follows the rose and saffron of a winter sunset. . . . What a beautiful sunset . . . it's just like a land in itself, isn't it? That long, low bank of purple cloud is the shore, and the clear sky further on is like a golden sea. . . . The sky faded out, but the strip of yellow along the western horizon grew brighter and fiercer, as if all the stray gleams of light were concentrating in one spot; the distant hill, rimmed with priest-like fire, stood out in dark distinctness against it. . . . The fine, empurpling dye of sunset still stained the western skies, but the moon was rising and the water lay like a great, silver dream in her light. . . . Beyond, the harvest hills were basking in an amber sunset radiance, under a pale, aerial sky of rose and blue. The distant spruce groves were burnished bronze, and their long shadows barred the upland meadows. . . . They all sat down in the little pavilion to watch an autumn sunset of deep red fire and pallid gold. . . . They lingered in the park until sunset, living in the amazing miracle and glory and wonder of the springtide. . . . The girls wandered down a long pineland aisle that seemed to lead right out into the heart of a deep-red, overflowing winter sunset . . . pausing in an open space where a rosy light was staining the green tips of the pines."

It was impossible for Maud to leave natural beauty well alone. With Anne she would cry, "Spring [or sunset, or sunrise, or autumn, or wind or moon or sea] is singing in my blood . . . I'm seeing visions and dreaming dreams." But then, this is part of her continuing appeal. She speaks for so many inarticulate people in the grip of emotions they cannot release, particularly the young for whom she writes who are making their own first discoveries about the joy of living.

She was aware of her failure to reach the heights. "I wanted to put something of the beauty I felt into the words of my poem," she says through Emily, "and now . . . the words seem flat and foolish and the picture I tried to draw in them not so wonderful after all. . . . It seems to me there is something beyond words—any words—all words—something that always escapes you when you try to grasp it—and yet leaves something in your hand which you wouldn't have had if you hadn't reached for it."

Nevertheless, some happy inspirations succeed in creating instant and unforgettable pictures. *A December fir wood . . . where I've heard harps swept by the fingers of rain and wind. . . . A little room . . . where old dreams hang thick . . . silky thin paper [from Japan] with dim cherry blossoms on it like ghosts. . . . Long hills scarfed with the shadows of autumnal clouds. Windy meadows harvest-deep.*

And Maud's work is leavened by laughter. She knew how to set down with risible effect small incidents from her own experience or her imagination—though she was indignant ("Gods, how I ground my teeth!") at a critic's suggestion that the incidents and droll sayings in *A Tangled Web* must have originated from many hours of talking with the old folk of the Island. Nevertheless, it is not to her discredit that she made clever use of much of her own experience in all her books. Milty Boulter's belief that heaven was in his Uncle Sam's garret came straight from her own childish location of heaven in the Clifton church attic. The child Davy's assumption that there would be jam in heaven surely came from an encounter with a real-life child's misreading (perhaps her own) of the catechism: *"Why should we love God? Because He makes* preserves *and redeems us.* Gog and Magog, endowed with the green spots of Grandfather Montgomery's china dogs, turn up in *Anne of the Island* at Patty's Place, on either side of the fireplace. And the mournful Methodist minister's wife of Maud's own childish writing buried her brood of children again from Newfoundland to Vancouver in Anne's story *My Graves.*

Some of the funny schoolroom episodes must have come straight from Maud's own teaching days, student howlers carefully jotted down in her bulging notebooks: Thomas à Becket canonized as *a snake*: the definition of honeymoon as "an extra nice kind of bicycle": of a glacier as "a man who puts in window frames." And she had a refreshing ability to bring soulful sentiment crashing back to earth with practical realism. "I like to lie in bed and hear [the rain] pattering on the roof and drifting through the pines," says poetic Anne. "I like it when it stays on the roof," replies her friend forthrightly. "It doesn't always."

Though she was furious at the unauthorized publication

of *Further Chronicles of Avonlea,* Maud should have been pleased by the introductory flattery about her one-sentence characterizations, followed by examples. There was Aunt Cynthia, who "always gave you the impression of a full-rigged ship coming gallantly on before a favourable wind"; the lady who was "good at having presentiments—after things happen"; the lady who "looked like a woman whose opinions were always very decided and warranted to wear."

The people in Maud's pages seldom stand alone; over the shoulder of each of them peer the faces of a dozen inquisitive neighbours, fascinated by the foibles of their fellows. James Baxter, who had stopped talking to his wife, "and *nobody knows why.*" Systematic Luke Elliot, who marked on a chart every New Year's day "all the days he means to get drunk on —*and sticks to it.*" Mrs Stirling, who "would sulk for days if offended, with the airs of an insulted duchess." Aunt Wellington, "who always enunciated commonplaces as if uttering profound and important truths." Mrs. Frederick, who ate her breakfast in sulky silence, "offended with Providence for sending a rainy day when she wanted to go to a picnic." And the generally accepted view in the society of which she wrote that "It was permissible, even laudable, to read to improve your mind and your religion, but a book that was enjoyable was dangerous."

No wonder young and old the world over delightedly recognized the silly and irritating taboos of their youth and the quirks of their associates in the figures of Maud's fictional world.

CHAPTER TWENTY-NINE

Green Gables
enshrined

The sequel to *Pat of Silver Bush* had been published in 1935 as *Mistress Pat* (Maud had wanted *The Chatelaine of Silver Bush*). She had undertaken it with her usual reluctance— "inspiration always goes after the first book." Reluctantly again, she started another Anne book, to appear as *Anne of Windy Poplars*. Again she lost her choice of title: she had wanted it to be *Anne of Windy Willows*, but though this title was used for the English edition (later, much to her delight, chosen as "the romantic book of the month" by the *Daily Mirror*), Canadian publishers evidently feared a confusion with Kenneth Grahame's *The Wind in the Willows*.

The book brought some unexpected dividends. For one sentence—"I was just moonlighted into thinking I loved him" —she was paid three dollars by *Reader's Digest* in 1937. "*That* was the *highest price* I was ever paid for a single line in my life!" In 1939, Twentieth Century Fox paid her $150 for the use of a title from a story she had incorporated into the same book, *The Man Who Wouldn't Talk*. Titles cannot be copyrighted, so the payment was a precautionary measure to avoid possible lawsuits; but "I have never made $150 so easily before," chortled Maud, "dying of curiosity" to see how the title would fit the eventual film.

She would sign a film contract of her own in 1939 with RKO for the rights to *Anne of Windy Poplars*, "after living in a hail of air-mail letters for two months. . . . Or rather, I signed *five* contracts, each in 19 different places—ninety-five times in all!!" The tightness of the contract had the kind of piquancy Maud would enjoy: once bitten, by the loss of the rights for *Anne of Green Gables*, she had learned to be twice shy in the matter of future dramatic rights.

In July 1936 she was doing the spadework on a book with a new heroine, Jane Stuart. The book, *Jane of Lantern Hill*, appeared a year later. Set partly in Toronto, but chiefly in Prince Edward Island, it was an idyllic Cinderella-story with a vindictive grandmother playing stepmother-and-ugly-sisters, and a delightful new-found father as stand-in for Prince Charming. It was the stuff of dreams-come-true, the repressed child blossoming in the care of an understanding companion in a delicious little house full of joys and delights. "Magic! Why, the place was simply jammed with magic. You were falling over magic." The title was dangerously near one of Nellie McClung's, *Leaves from Lantern Hill*, but Maud defiantly refused to change it. She had picked it, she said, before Mrs McClung's book appeared. Later she was intrigued to hear that a girl in Montreal had asked for "that Montgomery book *A Chain of Lantern Hills*."

For four years, Maud had not managed to get back to her Island. On a visit in October 1936 she found the old scenes unchanged, but many old friends were gone. Truly, she was "haunted by many ghosts." She was at first dubious about a plan to develop a national park embracing Cavendish and centred on *Green Gables*, now grown into a legend, though the house the tourists flock to see as Anne's Green Gables is not, specifically, the house Maud had in mind. *Her* Green Gables, she has explained, was in fact a composite of several dearly loved houses from her childhood. Nevertheless, for a fictional character, it does not seem out of place to have a fictional house, and enough of it is genuinely associated with the book to give it authority. The bedroom over the front door was Anne's room in Maud's mind. It is now equipped with furniture of Anne's period, chosen to fit as nearly as possible the description of her room in Maud's book. Lovers' Lane runs through the woods nearby, part of the farm then owned by Ernest Webb, whose wife was a Macneill and whose home, where Maud stayed for a few days on every visit, is now the house known as Green Gables. A daughter of the house, Anita Webb, lived with Maud in her Toronto home for several months in 1939-40, helping her with the management of the house.

But in 1936, Maud felt it was *"sacrilege"* to throw open to desecration by the public "all of those lanes and woods-encircled fields where I roved for years. . . . They will never —can never be the same to me again." Sensibly, however, she recognized that the government action had saved the area from being broken up and sold to individual and possibly uncaring owners, who might cut down the trees and destroy the lanes. "Now they are to be preserved exactly as they are."

"She was really very pleased and proud," says Miss Webb. "She was all set to listen to the broadcast when the park was opened officially—and nothing came through. When she telephoned the CBC, they had to tell her apologetically that there had been a blind spot in the transmission."

When she returned three years later, she felt even better about the project. All her old beloved haunts had been maintained, and new beauties added. Down a flight of stone steps she was charmed to find a cup hung on a birch tree for all who would drink from the water of the Dryad's Bubble, now surrounded by a stone wall.

In 1937 Maud was devastated by the death of her latest cat Good Luck. She had sat up with Lucky for three cold April nights six years before when the cat had double pneumonia: wrapped in a blanket by an open window for the fresh air the vet had said was imperative for recovery. Always, the latest cat seemed to have been the dearest, most lovable, most human of them all, but perhaps Lucky meant more to Maud than any of them. He had been (she told Weber) "for the greater part of five thousand nights and days my inseparable companion. . . . I loved other cats *as cats*. I loved Lucky as a *human being*. He was the most beautiful and uniquely marked cat I have ever seen, with *human* eyes. . . . Whatever Luck was he was *not* a cat. A cat's body, true! But it was not a cat soul that inhabited it . . . I buried him under a little pine tree in my rock garden and no cat was every more deeply missed or sincerely mourned." Maud's letters to MacMillan (also a cat-lover) are touchingly full of loving references to her pet, and her account of Luck's death ran to six heart-broken pages.

In mid-1937, her publishers, with *Jane* due to appear in a couple of months, had begun demanding another Anne book. Maud thought she might begin one, but her heart was not in it. Each month of the year had brought her new and depressing problems—"worry over many things, some of them the kind that can't be told to the world but must be hidden and not spoken of," wrote Maud to MacMillan. Ewan's health had continued to deteriorate. "It was more than nerves this time—for about two months in the summer he was a mental case, and among other symptoms, lost his memory completely. I could not bear to have him go to any institution for I knew no one could understand him as I did, for I have nursed him through so many of these attacks."

As a result of worrying, and following a debilitating attack of influenza in the winter of 1937-38, Maud herself had a nervous breakdown—that convenient term the doctors employ, she said sardonically, when they can't find out what is wrong. The will to work, her appetite, her ability to sleep all fled. She was obsessed by a dreadful restlessness—"for 4 months I lived in a sort of hell on earth"—walking the floor to try to gain control of her nerves. She endured the condition for four months before the autumn brought the beginning of improvement and, at last, in the spring of 1939, she found herself (stopping to rap on wood) better than she had felt for years. But "I shall never forget the terrible nights."

Maud had seen *Anne* turned into two three-act plays in 1937 (one by Alice Chadwicke, one by Wilbur Braun) without any reward to herself because of the loss of dramatic rights in her original contract. She felt the Chadwicke version was done "fairly well," but she had criticisms. She could not see puritan Marilla exclaiming "No siree!" She did not like "the silly and unnecessary love story" injected into the play. Anne would never have used big words improperly, especially when she was a grown-up college girl. But at a performance she had attended in a nearby centre, where "Josie Pye stole the show," Maud found Anne "capital," Matthew "excellent," Mrs Lynde "good though too thin," and Gilbert "a dreadful stick." The audience had seemed to enjoy it, however.

Fan mail was still coming to her from around the world. From the beginning she had heard from "men and women who are grandparents, boys at school and college, old pioneers in the Australian bush, missionaries in China, monks in remote monasteries, and red-haired girls all over the world . . . telling me how they loved Anne and her family." A letter from a woman in Jerusalem in 1939 about Jane had given Maud a thrill that reached far beyond its kindly comments, and set her imagination soaring. "To think of a book of mine being read in that ancient city where David and Solomon reigned and the Great Teacher worked. . . ." An odd little note came from a sixteen-year-old American girl to say that "the joy of life would be killed for her" if a rumour that the author of the books was married turned out to be true. Had she developed a passion for an L. M. Montgomery she believed to be a *man*?

CHAPTER THIRTY

World
upside down

Maud had started on what would be the last *Anne* book in September 1938, completing it in December by doing nothing else for the whole four months. Concerned with the baby days of Anne's children, it was published as *Anne of Ingleside* in 1939. Maud, who had been ill in August that year, spent a month in the Island and came back, as always, renewed. But she was on a downhill path. The outbreak of World War Two had further depressed her already low spirits. "I am not going to talk about the war," she wrote to Weber. "I can't! It is not *fair* that we who went through all this before should have to go through it again. That is childish, of course, but it is exactly how I feel."

With what horror, at the war's very beginning, did she open her paper on the morning of Monday, September 4, to read the savage story of the torpedoed *Athenia* and learn that among the unreported passengers was the Reverend William Allan, Jean's brother? With his son Andrew (to become known Canada-wide in later years as a top CBC broadcaster) and Andrew's fiancée Judith Evelyn, Mr Allan would have been on another, earlier ship, had not reluctance to leave his mother postponed his return. One of the survivors who crammed into an overloaded lifeboat, he was tossed into the sea when the propellor of a Norwegian rescue ship cut into the small craft, killing eighty who had escaped the original disaster. Did Maud, for Jean's sake, bring herself to attend the memorial service in Dovercourt Road Church in October, when hundreds stood in the aisles to join the fifteen hundred seated mourners and the hundreds more standing outside?

Neither of her sons was immediately threatened. Chester, who had given up mining engineering in favour of law, was rejected on account of shortsightedness, and Stuart, refused permission to join a medical unit by a Medical Council decree that held back all students not yet through their course, did not join the navy until after his mother's death. But the enormous waste and tragedy of war, added to her husband's deteriorating mental health, bowed her down. Ewan went to Florida in January 1940 hoping for improvement, and Maud, writing to Weber in February, was expecting him to stay until the end of March.

This was the last letter Maud wrote to Weber in her usual style of high courage. She did her best to hold onto the two good friends of half a lifetime, with whom she had explored ideas, discussed books, exchanged gossip, confided fears, shared a treasured communion of the spirit.

Through the year she tried to continue her writing, working on a sequel to *Jane of Lantern Hill* that would never be completed. In mid-1940 she had again become victim of a "dreadful nervous breakdown" that followed a bad fall and the depressing war news. She had injured her right arm, but she managed to send a letter to MacMillan in both July and August: not quite "notes," but not "real" letters either. In the August letter she was showing signs of her old resilience after her "intolerable distress. . . . I really think I have turned the corner. . . . Several things including my fall came all at once with the breaking of France and caused [my breakdown]. But now I really have some hope of recovering, things do not look so black. But even yet I very often wonder what God can be thinking about!!!"

At the end of December 1940 she wrote to Weber: "Dear Friend . . . I do not think I will ever recover. . . . Let us thank God for a long and true friendship." Three more letters would reach him, one of them merely a note from her nurse to thank him for the plant he had sent her, the others a few scrawled lines penned in hopeless dejection.

In 1941, MacMillan received five scribbled postcards, each more pathetic than the last. "I am no better. . . . I have had a very bad year. . . . We have lived to see beauty vanish from the world. . . . Am no better dear friend and never will be.

You do not know the blows that have fallen on my life for years. I tried to hide them from my friends. I feel my mind is going. . . . I am very ill and still not able to write."

For six months Maud struggled with what she had once called "all tears and fears that haunt the halls of night." By December 1941 only a hypodermic enabled her to write at all, and she penned her last letters to her two friends. And at last allowing her guard to drop, and stripped of all hope, she uncovered the torments with which she had so bravely coped throughout most of her marriage. To Weber she wrote on the 26th: "My husband is very miserable. I have tried to keep the secret of his melancholic attacks for twenty years, as people do not want a minister who is known to be such, but the burden broke me at last, as well as other things. And now the war. I do not think I will ever be well again."

And to MacMillan: "Thanks for your gift. I am no better and never will be. But I thank God for our long and beautiful friendship. Perhaps in some other incarnation in some other happier world we will renew it. This past year has been one of constant blows to me. My eldest son has made a mess of his life and his wife has left him. My husband's nerves are worse than mine even. I have kept the nature of his attacks from you for over 20 years but they have broken me at last. . . . I expect conscription will come in and they will take my second son and then I will give up all effort to recover because I shall have nothing to live for. May God bless you and keep you for many years. There are few things in my life I have prized as much as your friendship and letters. Remember me as I used to be and not as I am now. Yours in all sincerity and perhaps for the last time. . . ."

Long, long ago, she had written to Weber: "I . . . hope that death will come to me *suddenly*. I don't want to *know* it is coming. I envy those who die in their sleep." And later: "I have a horrible fear that I'll die by inches." Her fear was only too justified. For the last months of her life she watched death coming, in real agony of mind and spirit.

She died on April 24, 1942. Perhaps at this moment she was glad to lay down the terrible burden of living. Obituaries in Canadian newspapers were shorter than they would have been had not war now screamed from the front pages and column space limited their length; but most of them ran to several inches, usually with a portrait of the "beloved Canadian author." (*The Canadian Author and Bookman*, journal of the Canadian Authors Association for which she had done so much, so willingly, did not bother with an obituary until September 1944, reprinting a Canadian Press report from two and a half years before.)

Her sons and her husband accompanied her body to the Island where her spirit had always been, for burial in the little Cavendish cemetery on Wednesday, April 29; she would be joined nearly two years later by Ewan, who died in December 1943. "A great concourse of people" thronged the Presbyterian church or stood outside for Maud's memorial service. It was a day of windy sunshine, with snow still holding in patches and gulf ice visible in the distance. Some birds had returned already—wild geese, a few songbirds. The minister who had married her, the Reverend John Stirling, presided at her funeral: her poem about the Resurrection, *The Watchman*, was read, as well as extracts from *Chronicles of Avonlea*, "in support of the view that she was possessed of a mind of unusual range and soundness, and understood the evangelical as well as the cultural and ethical side of the appeal of the Gospel."

The Reverend Dr Frank Baird, representing the Moderator of the General Assembly of the Presbyterian Church in Canada, added his tribute. Among the many important and distinguished names adorning Island history, he said, "I do not think any will outshine the star that shone, and will continue to shine down through the ages in Lucy Maud Montgomery Macdonald. If service to Prince Edward Island be accepted as a criterion of judgment, if I mistake not, and I think posterity will concur—she places first . . . the palm for all the Maritimes should go to the distinguished authoress robed 'in the white majesty of death' [her own phrase] here before us today."

"What a strange thing this death is," she had written to Weber more than thirty years earlier. ". . . Theologians have done much to surround death with horror and dread. If we

187

listened to Nature's teachings we should be happier, truly believing (I hold) that death is simply a falling asleep, probably with awakening to some happy and useful existence, at the worst an endless and dreamless repose. Isn't the Christian (?) doctrine of eternal torment as *hellish* as the idea it teaches? . . . I admit that a consciousness of sin and remorse is a hell in itself. . . . Nobody wilfully chooses evil. . . . Sometimes, in the case of bad habits, we cannot turn from it. But I believe that only lasts while the physical body on which the habit is impressed lasts. When it is destroyed the habit will also be destroyed and the liberated soul will get 'another chance', with the warning of its bitter experiences."

In March 1931 she had written to MacMillan, "Yes, I suppose we must both face the fact that we are 'growing old'. ["I have got fat!" she had complained. "I weigh 150 lbs.—quite as much as my height can carry. . . . If it goes on I shall have to diet or exercise. For the first I have no liking . . . for the second no time."] For my own part I have never *felt* old till this past year. And I admit that several times during its passage I *have* felt rather wearily 'old'—as if courage had run low and there was little to look forward to in existence. This may have been merely the result of my poor health and if I were to recover fully I might not feel that way at all. And, in any event, I say to myself 'I believe in a series of re-incarnations. If that is true I am really nearing the time *when I will be young again.* Just as often after noonday we really get nearer to another morning with every passing minute.' Though, when I feel very tired I catch myself hoping there will be a good long restful *sleep* between the evening and the morning. As no doubt there will. What other truth is our night and sleep meant to teach us?"

Maud Macdonald had a talent for companionship that stood her in good stead when her whole being cried out to be alone, not to have to *mix* with people she did not much care for. But the rigid control demanded of her patience and temper, even though friendliness came naturally to her, doubtless contributed to those periods of nervous tension that finally overcame her.

Not many of us would be able to maintain the outward face of modesty Maud presented to the world after the accolades she received. She can be forgiven, or at least granted understanding, for an inward arrogance. And with the knowledge of her terrible private problems, we can forgive, perhaps even admire, the control that hid them from most of her neighbours and enabled her to receive the genuine admiration and love of the people of her congregations. This is no mean achievement for a tempestuous, contradictory personality that was at once critical and warm-hearted, forgiving and yet not a little spiteful, courageous and fearful, and perhaps above all else, loyal to her own personal code; but using the very human defence of self-mockery as a forearming against the darts of criticism from others that could all too easily hit their target.

Without doubt she felt tethered by the need to behave circumspectly (though it was no effort for her to behave with dignity). The respect she received as famous author, supplemented by her personal intelligence and charm, probably would have saved her from the kind of ungenerous and small-minded censure she had seen vented on other luckless ministerial wives. The *Open Letter from a Minister's Wife* she wrote in 1931 was based as much on her youthful observations of ready-to-pounce congregational attitudes in the ingrown little fundamentalist communities of the Island as on her own experience. "[The minister's wife] expects that the congregation will concede to her a right to her own opinions, tastes, methods of housekeeping and child training. To be the target of endless criticism along these lines would take the joy out of any life." She gave as example a minister who had been rejected by a congregation for no more reason than that his wife had been frivolous enough to turn up with a red rose in her hat. "Even if her dress were dowdy and her hat swore at her nose, she wouldn't be a bit the better wife to the minister or help to the congregation."

Yet of course there had been compensations for her. "I look back and see many lovely things. . . . Houses that always seemed pleased to have you come to them. Frank, ungrudging tributes, appreciative, priceless words that cast a sudden rainbow over existence. Dear gentle souls who never once made me feel that I had said the wrong thing. . . . Little friendly, neighborly offerings now and then—the jar of cream or jelly, the box of eggs, the root of an admired perennial. . . . And the dear, dear women I have known!"

But despite her huge and unexpected success, despite the "many lovely things" she could look back on, one is left with the feeling that Maud Macdonald did not find in life what she had so ecstatically expected in those golden days of her childhood. Possession of so rapturous a response to beauty is not always the enviable gift it seems to be when life allows no real control of one's destiny, and the "great peaks" so often mean "great depths" as well. In 1908, "circumstances over which I have no control" brought her morbid brooding. In 1923, she was "compelled . . . by the circumstances of my existence" to play the detested part of a "mixer." Was she too deeply indoctrinated to escape without guilt from an interpretation of religion she could not accept? Her heart told her that God was not the God her grandmother had directed her to, not the God of the tight-lipped holders-to-the-letter-of-the-Law, but she could not break free. She was bound inescapably to her early training, though she stirred restlessly within its straitjacket.

"She was very religious," writes her son, "although in a rather rigid way, and although in her writings she gave the impression of broad tolerance of human weaknesses, she did not condone any such elasticity in herself or in her family. I think she derived comfort and strength from her religion, but it was a rather bleak and forbidding one."

Man is a worshipping animal, she knew, and Maud Montgomery Macdonald's strength had to be derived from this knowledge. She had a worshipping soul that found only beauty fit to worship, and there was not enough of that. Like Anne, "If I really wanted to pray . . . I'd go out into a great big field all alone or into the deep, deep woods, and I'd look up into the sky . . . into that lovely blue sky that looks as if there was no end to its blueness. And then I'd just *feel* a prayer."

In many ways she found it a dark world, but she had the courage to whistle in the dark.

No wonder her Island rejuvenated her. All of Cavendish was a prayer. She could offer up a soul-ful of worship, from the days of wonder she had known there from her very first breath. Her cousin Ken, had she but realized it when he was a pesky small boy around their grandmother's home, was living out the same dream, to be stored away and brought out to be dreamed again when the years had moved ahead and the spirit needed refreshing. In 1974, one hundred years after she was born, nearly eighty years after his own birth, Ken Macneill would write with his cousin Maud's nostalgia of the Island's unbreakable spell.

I sometimes want to return to Cavendish again and sometimes I don't. I know I'll never find the kerosene lamps again, nor the tallow candles, nor the root cellars, not the giant built-in ice-boxes that farmers used to cut ice for and fill up each spring with sawdust, nor the all-dirt red roads . . . and the daily milk run to Stanley Bridge to the cheese factory, nor the voyages out a mile or two with my uncle in his dory, and a line and hook to get an odd mackerel or even a stray haddock, to say nothing about hauling up his half dozen or more lobster traps: or the sand-pipers on the beach which I flung pebbles at and never hit, or going to bed with a cup of molasses and water, nor the twelve-mile buggy trip from Hunter River station, twice a year, and Maudie's rat-tat-tat upstairs long after I went to bed, and climbing trees for cherries and apples, usually not quite ripe but so what, and my early morning arising to go to the brook and haul up a few four or five inch trout for breakfast. . . . All gone, and all enjoyed when it happened, and now we go there in an hour or so and in the air. . . .

Cavendish still has its magic. Maud was right—she never should have left it. But then perhaps she never really did.

Bibliography

Books by L. M. Montgomery (in order of first publication date):

Anne of Green Gables, L. C. Page & Co., Boston, 1908

Anne of Avonlea, L. C. Page & Co., Boston, 1909

Kilmeny of the Orchard, L. C. Page & Co., Boston, 1910

The Story Girl, L. C. Page & Co., Boston, 1911

Chronicles of Avonlea, L. C. Page & Co., Boston, 1912

The Golden Road, L. C. Page & Co., Boston, 1913

Anne of the Island, L. C. Page & Co., Boston, 1915

The Watchman & Other Poems, McClelland & Stewart, Toronto, 1916

Anne's House of Dreams, Frederick Stokes & Co., New York, 1917

Rainbow Valley, Frederick Stokes & Co., New York, 1919

Further Chronicles of Avonlea, L. C. Page & Co., Boston, 1920

Rilla of Ingleside, Frederick Stokes & Co., New York, 1921

Emily of New Moon, Frederick Stokes & Co., New York, 1923

Emily Climbs, Frederick Stokes & Co., New York, 1925

The Blue Castle, Frederick Stokes & Co., New York, 1926

Emily's Quest, Frederick Stokes & Co., New York, 1927

Magic for Marigold, Frederick Stokes & Co., New York, 1929

A Tangled Web, Frederick Stokes & Co., New York, 1931 (English title: *Aunt Becky Began It*)

Pat of Silver Bush, Frederick Stokes & Co., New York, 1933

Courageous Women (in collaboration with Marian Keith and Mabel Burns McKinley), McClelland & Stewart, Toronto, 1934

Mistress Pat, Frederick Stokes & Co., New York, 1935

Anne of Windy Poplars, Frederick Stokes & Co., New York, 1936 (English title: *Anne of Windy Willows*)

Anne of Ingleside, Frederick Stokes & Co., New York, 1939

Jane of Lantern Hill, Frederick Stokes & Co., New York, 1937

The Road to Yesterday, McGraw-Hill Ryerson, Toronto, 1974 (Posthumous publication)

Arranged in chronological sequence of Anne's life the complete series is as follows:

Anne of Green Gables (1908): Anne's childhood.

Anne of Avonlea (1909): Anne as teacher.

Anne of the Island (1915): Anne goes to college.

Anne of Windy Poplars (1936): Love letters to Gilbert Blythe during her term as school principal.

Anne's House of Dreams (1918): Marriage and first child.

Anne of Ingleside (1939): Birth of five more children.

Rainbow Valley (1919): The children grow up.

Rilla of Ingleside (1921): Anne's daughter and the war years.

Short pieces by L. M. Montgomery:

"On Cape Le Force" (poem), Charlottetown *Daily Patriot*, November 26, 1890

"A Western Eden," Prince Albert *Times*, June 17, 1891

"A Girl's Place at Dalhousie College," Halifax *Herald*, April 29, 1896

"The 'Teen-Age Girl," *Chatelaine*, March 1931

"An Open Letter from a Minister's Wife," *Chatelaine*, October 1931

Various poems and short stories (some of which were reprinted in *Chronicles* and *Further Chronicles of Avonlea*) in such publications as *Everybody's, McClure's, Canadian Magazine, Chatelaine, Maclean's, Delineator, The Criterion, Youth's Companion, Forward, The Congregationalist, Christian Advocate*)

"The Alpine Path," *Everywoman's World*, Toronto, 1917

Articles about L. M. Montgomery:

Campbell, Hon. Thane. "Address at Cavendish on the unveiling of a memorial in memory of L. M. Montgomery," September 12, 1948

Chapman, Ethel. "The Author of Anne," *Maclean's* Magazine, 1919.

Fitzpatrick, Helen. "Anne's First Sixty Years," *Canadian Author and Bookman*, Spring, 1969.

Hill, Maude Petitt. "The Best Known Woman in Prince Edward Island," *Chatelaine*, May and June 1928.

Pacey, Desmond. *Creative Writing in Canada*, Toronto, 1952

Phelps, A. L. *Canadian Writers*, Toronto, 1951

Presbyterian Record. Obituary, June 1942

Sclanders, Ian. "Lucy of Green Gables," *Maclean's* Magazine, December 15, 1951

Weber, Ephraim. "L. M. Montgomery as a Letter Writer," *Dalhousie Review*, October 1942

Weber, Ephraim. "L. M. Montgomery's 'Anne,' " *Dalhousie Review*, April 1944

Newspapers (relevant years):

Alloa Journal
Charlottetown *Daily Patriot*
Charlottetown *Examiner*
Charlottetown *Guardian*
Halifax *Herald*
Halifax *Chronicle*
Manitoba Evening Free Press
Montreal *Star*
Ottawa *Citizen*
Prince Albert *Daily News*
Prince Albert *Times*
Saskatchewan, The
Saskatchewan *Herald*
Toronto *Globe*
Toronto *Globe and Mail*
Toronto Star

Other sources:

Bolger, Francis W. P. (ed.). *Canada's Smallest Province.*

P.E.I.: The Prince Edward Island 1973 Centennial Commission.

——. *The Years before "Anne."* P.E.I.: The Prince Edward Island Heritage Foundation, 1975.

Bulwer-Lytton, E. *Zanoni.* London: Chapman & Hall, 1853.

Eggleston, Wilfrid. *The Green Gables Letters.* Toronto: Ryerson Press, 1960.

——. *While I Still Remember,* Toronto: Ryerson Press, 1968.

Historical Sketch: 100th Anniversary, Leaskdale, Ontario: St. Paul's Presbyterian Church, 1962.

Historical Sketch of Norval Presbyterian Church, Centennial 1938

Holland, Norah M. *Spun-Yarn and Spindrift.* London and Toronto: J. M. Dent, 1918.

Lockhart, A. J. *The Papers of Pastor Felix.* Toronto: William Briggs, 1903.

L. M. Montgomery as Mrs. Ewan Macdonald of The Leaskdale Manse, 1911-1926. Leaskdale, Ontario: St Paul's Presbyterian Women's Association, 1965.

Lucy Maud Montgomery, The Island's Lady of Stories. Springfield, Prince Edward Island: The Women's Institute, 1963.

Meacham's Atlas of Prince Edward Island (1880). Reprinted Mika Publishing Co., Belleville, Ontario: 1973.

MacMillan, George Boyd. Letters from L. M. Montgomery (unpublished).

Opie, Iona and Peter. *Children's Games in Street and Playground,* Oxford at the Clarendon Press, 1969.

Public Archives of Canada. RG—15, B1, Box 1089, file 137340.

Ridley, Hilda M. *L. M. Montgomery.* Toronto: Ryerson Press, 1956.

Simpson, Harold. *Cavendish: Its History, Its People.* Truro, 1973.

Wallace, F. W. *Wooden Ships and Iron Men.* London: Hodder & Stoughton, 1925.

Watson, Albert Durrant (ed.). *The Twentieth Plane.* Philadelphia: G. W. Jacobs & Co., 1919.

Weber, Ephraim. Letters from L. M. Montgomery (unpublished), PAC: MG 30 D 36.

Index

199